ENSNARED BY HIS WORDS

Ensnared by His Words

My Chaucer Obsession

Dolores L. Cullen

FITHIAN PRESS, MCKINLEYVILLE, CALIFORNIA, 2008

Copyright © 2008 by Dolores L. Cullen
All rights reserved
Printed in the United States of America

Published by Fithian Press
A division of Daniel and Daniel, Publishers, Inc.
Post Office Box 2790
McKinleyville, CA 95519
www.danielpublishing.com

Distributed by SCB Distributors (800) 729-6423

LIBRARY OF CONGRESS CATALOGING-IN-PUBLICATION DATA
Cullen, Dolores L., (date)
  Ensnared by his words : my Chaucer obsession / by Dolores L. Cullen.
    p. cm.
  ISBN-13: 978-1-56474-472-2 (pbk. : alk. paper)
  ISBN-10: 1-56474-472-8 (pbk. : alk. paper)
  1. Cullen, Dolores L., (date) 2. Literary historians—United States—Biography.
3. Critics—United States—Biography. 4. Medievalists—United States—Biography. 5. Chaucer, Geoffrey, d. 1400—Influence. I. Title.
  PR55.C86A3 2008
  821'.1—dc22
  [B]
            2008000705

*In memory of
Judith Ann Wenrick
and
for her family
and her students*

ACKNOWLEDGEMENTS

I wish to extend my never-ending gratitude for help and encouragement to my family—first generation, second generation, and extended; to my friends, old and new; and to the members of the San Dimas Writers' Group, past and present. You've made a world of difference.

*Do not go where the path may lead,
go instead where there is no path,
and leave a trail.*

—*Ralph Waldo Emerson*

Contents

Foreword by Clare Asquith 13

I. Chicago and Points West 17

II. Enter Chaucer 25

III. Until One Is Committed 55

IV. Write a Book? 67

V. Virginia Hamilton Adair 79

VI. Search for a Publisher 89

VII. The 600th Year 123

VIII. Reactions 139

IX. Retro-Revelation! 147

X. What Now—and Why? 151

Foreword

It is tempting, but unwise, to underestimate the work of Dolores Cullen. Her direct style, her unaffected enthusiasm for the obscure reaches of Middle English, her openly celebratory approach to Chaucer as the poet who changed her life—this kind of thing is anathema to modern English literature scholars. As a result, most of them dismiss her startling theory that modern scholarship consistently overlooks something fundamental about the way Chaucer wrote. It is a theory that would be controversial even if it were presented in the jargon of professional academics. Luckily for us, she tells it straight, in language aimed at the common reader. The result is that we can share something of the excitement with which she stumbled into the shadowy, cosmic realms she believes are hidden within *The Canterbury Tales*.

A quick look at the accounts of her "eureka moments" in this gripping autobiography can be deceptive. They are not vague psychic intuitions. They arise from an obsessive, long-term saturation in the language and the history of the fourteenth century, in particular the language of allegory. For most modern scholars, allegory is an unappealing, moralizing, reductionist genre, positively damaging to the study of great works of literature like *The Canterbury Tales*. "I hate allegory," confessed one of the professors who rejected her thesis. But for Dolores Cullen, rich and continuous strands of double meaning are the life-blood of medieval literature. With insight and clarity she transposes the complex ancient theories of allegory into contemporary terminology, reviving in the process the "delight" which thinkers like Augustine considered essential to this neglected form of writing. In doing so, she provides convincing evidence that there is indeed a concealed, visionary dimension to Chaucer's work which has been neglected for centuries. She maintains that the Pilgrims are not merely a motley crowd of fourteenth century travelers. Oblique clues would have led Chaucer's humanist contemporaries to recognize a grand procession of familiar archetypes behind the lively, jostling pilgrimage to Canterbury. Cullen revives the Augustinian delight with which they would have related each of these everyday characters and their stories to aspects of the deepest of Christian mysteries. If she is right, a profound meditation on the relationship between the human and the divine lies at the heart of *The Canterbury Tales*.

This book recounts the moving story of a life to which this academic journey gave ultimate and unexpected meaning. The thrill of the early discovery of Chaucer's hidden level, the excitement of the detective trail through libraries, the shock of rejection, the dogged determination to fight for her corner, the sense of Chaucer as a living presence in her life, the joy of finding scholarly and family support in her darkest hours, the final, calm sense of completion—all this is narrated simply and humorously, and is set in the homely context of marriage, illness, friendship, the death of her husband, the births of her great-grandchildren. But her academic achievement goes beyond that of most eager amateur scholars. It is possible that she has alerted us, not simply to the pleasures of reading medieval literature on many levels, weighing and enjoying the nuances of each word, but to something even more fascinating: a deliberately deniable, enigmatic, allegorical wavelength to which the cultivated elite all over Europe resorted in times of religious corruption and repression. Some of the ideas Cullen detects within *The Canterbury Tales* would have been considered dangerous in Chaucer's day. The vividly human figure she identifies as Christ, for instance, traveling unrecognized in the company of the Pilgrims, would have horrified those who were too unsophisticated or too rigidly orthodox to appreciate the learned spirituality that inspired it. Cullen's books, unpretentious though they may seem, invite us to develop the forgotten cast of mind needed to tune into such a wavelength. Not surprisingly, this account of how they came to be written takes the reader on an utterly exhilarating literary adventure.

—Clare Asquith
Somerset, England
author of *Shadowplay*

ENSNARED BY HIS WORDS

I.

Chicago and Points West

A GREAT MANY OF my most cherished memories come from schooldays in Chicago on the great South Side. School was my favorite place; teachers my favorite people. And, as long as I can remember, a little voice inside of me that had never heard the name *Chaucer*, whispered, "Someday you are going to do something special."

The block I lived on, near Archer and Kedzie, had a row of ten or twelve small frame cottages, and a few brick two-flat buildings besides. The two-flats were owned by determined, hard-working Polish families. Almost everyone on the block had jobs in the manufacturing district across 47th Street. A short walk put you in the midst of factories, warehouses, a railroad yard with a roundhouse, and—next to that rail line—a tall grain elevator. The grain elevator is particularly memorable because it caught fire by spontaneous combustion and spewed smoke for weeks.

Our street was unpaved, just dirt with a layer of gravel over top. No parks had been planned for the area, but vacant lots—which we called *prairies*—were all we kids needed to exercise our imaginations. Sometimes it rained, or snow thawed, and water flooded the prairies. Then, if the temperature fell below freezing, we had a neighborhood ice skating rink!

On hot summer evenings, you could see youngsters carrying little tin buckets headed for the corner tavern to fetch beer for their dads. The tavern owner, who knew all the kids, would fill the pail and put it on the family's tab.

My recollections are not necessarily all happy. Our generally peaceful street erupted on September 1, 1939, when the news came over the radio that Hitler had marched into Poland. Old Mr. and Mrs. Reinhardt were suddenly identified with this Nazi invasion. The Poles (and their sympathizers) dragged stinking trash cans to the Reinhardt house. They dumped smelly, rotting garbage all over the "enemy's" garden, hollering Polish expressions all the while, and shaking their fists toward the house. Johann and Heidi, up until then, had been well-liked by everyone.

There were threats of diseases we no longer fear. Two of the Jankowski children—Stanley and Loretta—died from tuberculosis. It also claimed the life of my friend Peter Bartoshuk's father. And sometimes city schools were closed because of polio epidemics.

I attended Gunsaulus Grammar School eight blocks from home. School was always exciting for me. And so was that little voice that whispered, "Someday you are going to do something special." Maybe everyone feels that way, but it seemed as if part of me sat watching every opportunity that came along—examining, evaluating, silently asking, "Is this the moment, the turning point?" It gave a sense of animation to my everyday activities.

Though this blue-collar neighborhood lived with financial limits of the Depression, our teachers provided us with many wonders of the world. In 1937, for example, when the first panda in the United States—Su Lin—came to live at the Brookfield Zoo, in a suburb of Chicago, our entire school traveled on double-decker buses to see him.

Miss Tanney's sister, an airline stewardess (when air travel was rare), brought us silkworms from Japan. We gathered leaves from mulberry trees to feed them. The tiny black caterpillars quickly grew into fat, smooth, segmented white worms thicker than our fingers! We dunked the cocoons they made into boiling water and unwound the 2000-foot strand of silk from each cocoon onto a rotating frame. Though we learned that the boiled worm could be eaten, we declined the unique delicacy.

In Miss Heikes' class, if we had our required work finished and our desks clear by ten or fifteen minutes before three o'clock dismissal, she rewarded us by reading a portion of "Rikki Tikki

Tavi" from Kipling's *Jungle Book*, or an episode of mythology from the "Labors of Hercules."

For Miss Rutledge, a descendant of Edward Rutledge, a signer of the Declaration of Independence, U. S. history held personal importance.

Many of us saw the exhibit of Italian masterpieces on loan to the Art Institute. From Mrs. Canty, our art teacher, we learned proper manners regarding sculptures of *nude* figures. They demonstrated the beauty of the human body, and under no circumstances were we to giggle or point our fingers.

Children whose parents valued music and could afford the twenty-five cent price of admission attended children's concerts founded by Frederick Stock, conductor of the Chicago Symphony Orchestra. Our seats were at the top of the highest balcony in Orchestra Hall. Dr. Stock introduced each piece of music and we watched the orchestra perform far below us.

I wrote little articles about our field trips and projects for our school newspaper. Students, with a faculty advisor hovering over us, assembled stories and drawings that made up the entire dummy we sent to the printer. This after-hours activity pleased me greatly because it meant extra time at school.

And in eighth grade, we studied the history of Chicago. I went all out on the project—as I usually did—putting in countless hours collecting pictures, poems, and news articles. My "Chicago Book" contained no fewer than 150 pages!

High school held an even greater level of excitement. We were preparing to be adults. I registered for the College Prep curriculum—even though no one in my family had ever gone to college. Latin was my first experience with a foreign language. And I enjoyed the math sequence, especially geometry; the problems were like puzzles with a hidden clue.

Chemistry opened a whole new world. Mr. Schmidt demonstrated, for instance, how a cotton ball would sink immediately when placed on the liquid surface of a "wetting agent." (Not many years later wetting agents became the basis for detergents that replaced Lux Flakes and Rinso.) We memorized valences of the elements on the periodic table, worked out equations of chemical reactions, and learned that the *atom* is the smallest unit of matter.

As a sophomore I took the entrance exam for the accelerated program of studies at the University of Chicago. I passed, but my score didn't rate a scholarship. It's just as well.

(I took that test on the campus of the University of Chicago in the fall of 1942, in the midst of World War II. Much later, I would find out that only a few days and a short distance had separated me from the site of the very first, top secret, atomic chain reaction. The rules of chemistry were changing even as we learned them from Mr. Schmidt.)

In my final year of high school, I worked on the yearbook staff producing silk screen pages, which were a new endeavor that year. I'd taken many extracurricular courses and had sufficient credits to graduate in three and a half years. That pleased my folks because my father had a job offer out west and we planned to leave Chicago. Those plans were dropped, however, when the war ended suddenly.

Still in Chicago, just a year after graduating from Kelly High School, I met Ted Cullen and married him. Although marriage often puts an end to college dreams, marrying Ted is what made college possible. That little voice went silent, but remained vigilant. Patience would be the watchword.

❦

Now *fast forward*—It's 1965 and we're in Claremont, California. Ted, my husband, is a math professor at the nearby state college. The youngest of our four children has just started high school.

In the intervening years I had the thrill of hiking the Grand Canyon—down Bright Angel and up Kaibab, a twenty mile trek in a day. And while my children were in school, I did my share of playground monitoring and PTA jobs; helped with church activities; made cake and coffee for a little music group that met at our house on Friday evenings; sewed dolls for my three daughters and quilts for all of us—in the beginning from financial necessity, later for the joy of creativity.

Now with all my children independent, or nearly so, the demands on my time had diminished. I wondered how much sewing and gardening and baking it would take to keep life interesting and creative. That's when my husband asked what I would think of going to college. A rhetorical question, of course. What would I think? Nobody ever got applications and transcripts gathered together more quickly, in those long ago days before fax. The little voice became alert and attentive once again.

I registered as an English major, at California State Polytechnic College, where my husband taught. (It later became "University." Everyone refers to the campus as "Cal Poly.") I found every class, including those of General Ed, fascinating. I gained a different view of the business world, for example, from a survey of economics. Philosophy, biology, sociology, ceramics—every subject added new facets to my thinking. In my major, I proceeded through creative writing, survey courses of British and American literature, Milton, Shakespeare, and I would eventually take the required Chaucer course.

When my college days began, I knew Chaucer's name and that he had written the *Canterbury Tales*. That's all. How that information came to me, I have no idea. There had been no mention of him in high school. In a college survey course, he had made a fleeting appearance with the text in Modern English. The teacher, Mr. Shrager, saw no point in *burdening* students with Chaucer's Middle English. We read about the Wife of Bath, who had had five husbands. Mr. Shrager called her an "image of fruitfulness." Pondering her fruitfulness, I had to ask a question. (I had never hesitated to ask questions of teachers. After all, they wanted to help us, inform us, didn't they?) If the Wife is a *fruitful* image, why are there no children? "You are only *assuming* she has no children," he responded.

True, but wouldn't the author allude to them? It seemed a strange "omission." And, if no children are associated with her, why does she seem *fruitful?* Chaucer's allotted class periods passed without the opportunity to dig deeper into the matter. Then, on to a survey of Shakespeare.

After taking several other English courses, the time came to register for the class devoted *entirely* to Chaucer. The text was in Middle English, that is, English as spoken in 1400. And, the professor announced that all the tests would be in Middle English. We were expected to do the well-nigh impossible! Hadn't the survey teacher held the old language to be a pointless burden? This caused me (and my fellow students) some concern.

I forced myself out of the initial panic, however, by remembering I had once mastered chemical valences and Latin conjugations and declensions. Middle English would be the new challenge. The professor, Dr. Thomas Elliott, gave tips on pronunciation and recommended we read the assignments aloud.

Reading aloud proved to be a problem. I fell behind, so I bought a paperback of a modern version of the *Canterbury Tales* in order to catch up. But the modern lines lacked the complexity of Middle English—a great disappointment. I'll deal with that disappointment shortly.

As a compromise regarding the assignments, I did use the Middle English text, but gave up reading aloud. Referring often to the glossary, I became comfortable with the vocabulary. Patterns, such as, "likynge" and "holdynge" are *liking* and *holding;* "arwe" and "widwe" are *arrow* and *widow;* "suggestioun" and "impressioun" are *suggestion* and *impression*. All were easily recognizable. It felt rather like reading a dialect. Now, an odd thing began to happen. Chaucer's story created pictures in my mind that were *double*. Reading had never put double images in my mind's eye before. The phenomenon, I decided, had to come from the way Chaucer uses words. I knew allegories were highly valued in the Middle Ages and wondered if these were mental images of a story told on two levels simultaneously. I was intrigued.

Now, about that disappointment. Here is just one example. Chaucer says of one of his Pilgrims:

> There was no door that he could not heave off its hinges, or break it at running with his head.

That wild dynamic picture is lost when the Modern English version says:

> ...he would *boast*
> He could heave any door off hinge and post,
> Or take a run and break it with his head.

Chaucer didn't say he *boasted;* he said he *did* it! Chaucer's image holds super strength and recklessness. The Pilgrim in the modern adaptation is only a braggart.

For the required research paper, I wanted to learn more about the complex images. Scanning volume after volume of Chaucer criticism, I found no mention of this tantalizing feature. I'd ask Dr. Elliott for help.

We chatted briefly, during his office hour, before we got to the purpose of my visit. I explained about the images I saw. There seemed to be a surface story with hints of a second story unfolding simultaneously. I wanted to investigate this for my paper, but no scholar I perused touched on the idea. He asked if I saw Chaucer's work as an allegory. Is that what I meant? Yes, that was it, I replied.

Sun streamed through the office window. He leaned back in his swivel chair, fingertips of one hand poised against those of his other hand and, with an indulgent smile, said, "You are having problems finding such references because Chaucer *did not write allegory.*"

I had begun to feel that the double images were part of the *something special* I would do. I had no reason to think it would be easy. Professor Elliott's declaration initiated the element of frustration that would parallel the joy and excitement of a lifelong pursuit. At this point, I had not met Virginia Hamilton Adair. She would be, for me, a gift of inspiration and sustenance.

II.

Enter Chaucer

THE PICTURES IN MY HEAD remained, in spite of the professor's disbelief. The Pilgrims continued to pass in review from some part of my brain, without breaking stride. With them came the perpetual question: Why precisely *that* combination of characters?

An "open letter" I wrote in 1971 clarifies: *"In the beginning, it was all exciting and amazing, and I was eager, when I found the time, to share my ideas with others who knew Chaucer's works. (I must immediately add that 'my ideas' in the previous sentence in* no *way implies any creativity on my part. The ideas are perceptions of the Chaucer imagination and not at all to be confused with, or credited to my thinking.)"*

What an experience! Some mornings I would waken before my alarm went off. Ideas were clattering into my mind. I would, literally, jump out of bed, grab a pencil, try to catch and record all of them while they were "in view." I felt they would be irretrievable, if they weren't written down. They might never come again. (I still feel that way.)

The double images that came with reading shared my mind's eye with another area that watched Chaucer's Pilgrims in their endless loop. My days had become strange and exhilarating. I dearly wanted to talk to someone about it. Dr. Alex Chorney, the man who taught Chaucer before the new medievalist (Dr. Elliott) arrived, seemed a possibility. Being student-centered, his office door was always open. He motioned to me to sit down, and listened with attention. Finding this opportunity to share some of these happenings helped keep my excitement under control. He surprised and rather pleased me when he said I might be an "enfant terrible."

[26] Ensnared by His Words

Dr. Chorney's words encouraged me, but, I had to limit the library time spent on Chaucer. My journal entry tells the story. *"My curiosity was (and is) boundless. Each fact I uncovered made me want to know more and more in several directions all at once. It was wonderful—and frustrating."*

Of course, a good deal of stimulation and revelation came with simply reading more of Chaucer. A few days after my initial visit to Dr. Chorney, I dropped in on him again. Now, sure of the Host's hidden identity, I told him how Chaucer's words show that the guide of the Pilgrims is Christ. A Host providing the best food and strong wine for pilgrims on a journey draws upon poetic expressions regarding the Eucharistic Host of the Catholic Mass—a dominant force in Chaucer's lifetime. (As time went on, I would find numerous echoes defining this identity throughout the Host's associations with the characters.) Professor Chorney fidgeted impatiently. He saw this as "pigeon-holing" the poet as a religious propagandist. I asserted that, rather than *limiting* the poet, what I saw gave his work an added dimension. Critics who say Chaucer "lacks high seriousness" are proven wrong. And the complexity of the plan demonstrates the poet's even greater skill than had previously been acknowledged. The professor did not agree, but we parted amicably.

After a week or so of living with the parade of images and the murmuring query, "Why *this* combination of pilgrims?"—something astonishing happened. Suddenly, I had the answer. I saw *why* and I saw *who*. Why did the images appear double? Who are the alternate images? The Pilgrims meshed with signs of the zodiac and the personalities of planets all in the guise of pilgrims. I sat spellbound as each piece fit into place.

I had to tell someone about this flash of insight or I'd burst. Thank goodness my husband was home. I blurted out the amazing news to Ted, then grabbed my textbook to examine Chaucer's words. How had he concealed this? Why isn't it readily understood?

It isn't intended to be immediately understood because the reader is expected to *work* to gain the second meaning of an allegory. How could I confirm the celestial identities from his words? That word-search is unforgettable. Going line by line through the descriptions of the Pilgrims, I found one whose eyes twinkle like stars on a frosty night; he's Aries, a winter sign with a pair of prominent stars in the head of the constellation. Another Pilgrim has a curious gold pin under his chin; he's Leo, with a giant yellow star in his mane. And there is Taurus, the most easily recognized pilgrim by his physical description, with another bright yellow star that Chaucer disguises as "a thumb of gold." The woman whose motto is "Love conquers all" fits the planet Venus. The man dedicated to war is Mars. That's just a smattering of the numberless details Chaucer has hidden. All the combined—double—images is a subject to return to later. (And later, there would also be a bigger *why*. Why had Chaucer chosen to do this? But current happenings so captivated me that I couldn't think beyond them at the time.)

What a lot of news I would have for friendly Dr. Chorney. I could hardly contain myself as I began to tell of the previous evening's epiphany. (The professor's office partner got up and left.) I had just begun to compare the Pilgrims with the constellations when Professor Chorney leaned forward and frowned, interrupting my stream of enthusiasm. He quietly but firmly said, "Mind your humility." (Years later I would understand our sequence of conversations to have a darker, more serious atmosphere.)

His words caused something inside me to freeze. I thanked him for his time and excused myself. His final thrust brought me to tears. I just managed to get out into the hallway before they came streaming down my face. I met Ted by our car, and we left for home. As we drove, I told him how my attempt to be enlightening had suddenly been short-circuited. He and I had hoped Dr. Chorney would prove a mentor, but the hope dissolved almost as soon as it had appeared.

I felt closed in a box by his words. You don't hide Chaucer's images in a box. This dark, stifling atmosphere is foreign to the splendid creativity. I would have to burst open that box; let in the light; give his words fresh air.

Dr. Chorney and I each had a problem to consider. I'm sure he meant to put me in my place, remind me that a lowly undergraduate did not qualify to have an "original" thought. I could do nothing about *his* problem. End of that consideration. And, truth to tell, the pictures I told him about had *originated* with Chaucer, not with me.

Now for my problem: If I continued to alienate the English faculty one by one, how could I get through the rest of the quarter and, ultimately, through my senior year and graduate? What to do?

First, I had to look at the recommendation for "humility." I don't take it to mean self-effacement. Humility is based on truth. If Jascha Heifetz, the world-famous violinist wanted to be humble, he wouldn't say, "I'm a third-rate violinist." That would be a downright lie. If he said, "I'm very good, but not perfect," that is truth; *and* it's humility.

So, I figured truth for me is that I'm filled with complex pictures conceived by the first great English writer. Why or how, I don't know. A second and troublesome part of my humble truth, at that time, had to do with my poor writing skills. The job ahead of me, then, would be to learn to communicate what I see so other people can see it too. I had confidence in what I saw, even if I had not yet been able to demonstrate the phenomenon to others. I determined to ask for help, even if my questions appeared to be foolish. Asking "foolish" questions had never bothered me. It's often the only way to make progress.

Now, I had no doubt that doing *something special* involved Chaucer's Pilgrims. And I also had no doubt that it would not be easy, but that didn't matter. It was impossible NOT to pursue this Chaucer adventure.

With this debate inside of me, and exciting thoughts tumbling into my head whenever they chose, I had to remind myself that the Chaucer course had really just begun. Making friends with the language, seeing the double images, recognizing the Host, and now identifying the Pilgrims had all happened in rapid succession.

I had to get organized to start the required research paper.

What subject would I choose? The Wife of Bath, and her image as *fruitful*, ought to be a lively topic. I would try to discover why a possibly childless woman could be seen as fruitful.

With the work I did for that paper, I discovered her to be the *promise* of fruitfulness, the epitome of the life-force. Dr. Elliott completely rejected this point of view. His comments on the last page of my paper were abrasive. Using poor judgment, I tore them off and threw them away. Soon afterward, I regretted the action, realizing I had to learn to take harsh criticism. I never destroyed opinions after that. (There would be a great deal more to say about the Wife; a long, more satisfactory examination of the Wife is part of a book I would write.)

Research I had done for the Wife made me feel like I *wanted to*, like I *had to*, know everything about the time Chaucer lived. With barely enough time, during this quarter, to keep up with assignments for all my classes, I had little time to do extra reading about Chaucer's world. My husband had the answer to the time element. He gave me a 1971 birthday gift—of TIME. Instead of leaving campus every Friday at three o'clock, taking the bus home, and fixing dinner for his arrival at 7 P.M., I spent three and a half hours (3 to 6:30 P.M.) at the library each Friday, for the rest of the quarter, digging into any and all subjects that applied to the fourteenth century. Then we'd go out to dinner and, best of all, he'd listen while I told him all the things I'd just learned. What more could I want!

Some Fridays I read about the Black Plague (in one attack during Chaucer's childhood 50,000 Londoners died within a few months), sometimes about the Hundred Years War (Chaucer served in the English army against the French in an on-again-off-again war that began before his birth and lasted until long after his death), Gnosticism (the Gnostic religion sought mystical knowledge and held matter to be evil), Gothic cathedrals (Chaucer would have seen many being built during his travels), the Great Schism (rivalry between two popes—one in Rome, one in Avignon—remained unresolved while Chaucer lived), or the Inquisition (heretics on the Continent were persecuted, some being burned at the stake). My trail of interests branched in many directions and was endless. All this and more defined Chaucer's basic day-to-day existence.

The reading provided a lot of information, but, at the same time, each answer begot another question. No telling where it would all lead, but the journey had already begun.

It would also be advisable to find a topic for my Senior Project, a substantial research paper required for graduation. If, by the end of this school year, I had chosen my subject, I'd have all summer to do the necessary reading. Professor Lillian Wilds, who had recently received her doctorate, had been suggested as my advisor. I told her I preferred to work on Chaucer's double images, some of which I'd identified as zodiac figures. She listened to my unorthodox statements, then asked me to write a one-page example for her to look at, and she'd get back to me.

I chose the Prioress and the Monk as illustrations, showing how she fit the planet Venus, and he the constellation of Leo. I included a tentative list of all the Pilgrims and their possible astrological counterparts. I put the overview in her box the next day. A week later we talked.

When I arrived at her office, she greeted me with a cheery smile. As she returned my one page, she said, "I showed this to my doctoral advisor. He said you don't understand the fourteenth century well enough or you wouldn't have come up with these ideas." Then she added, "My suggestion is that you choose three women from the *Canterbury Tales* and compare and contrast them for your Project."

I thanked her and said I'd think about it. I was angry, though I tried not to let it show. After all, I might have to work with her and I couldn't afford to offend her at the outset. I didn't know whether my anger sprang from her showing my ideas to someone else without my permission—or if it came from her commonplace suggestion to compare three women. I had given her a recipe for a sumptuous bread pudding and she offered me dry toast, instead.

As I walked away from her office, I noticed that Dr. Ware's door stood ajar, and he sat at his desk, alone. I asked if he had time for a chat, and added that I didn't really need a professor; I needed a friend. He invited me in. I'm sure he could sense my irritation. I asked, "Do I *really* have to compare three women from the *Canterbury Tales* for my Senior Project?"

He appeared on the verge of chuckling as he countered with, "What else did you have in mind?"

He said, as chairman he had the option of being my advisor, if he chose. It would depend on my subject matter. Having enjoyed two courses with him, I said I would try to find an agreeable topic. I quickly made the decision to avoid the *Canterbury Tales* for the Project. There would be time for them after graduation.

That summer, in order to find a subject for the Senior Project, I read everything Chaucer had written except the *Canterbury Tales*. I finally settled on the *Parlement of Foules*. It has 700 lines—not too much, not too little—and complex double imagery. When I offered that title, Dr. Ware accepted it and became my advisor.

In September 1971, I took the bibliography class that helps students form a plan and set limits for their Senior Project. By pure serendipity Mrs. Virginia Hamilton Adair taught the class. (Without Mrs. Adair, what has become my lifelong adventure would have been a brief encounter with a medieval genius, and nothing more.) She had each student fill out a 3x5 card with a working title and a list of sources for their materials. When she handed back my card, there were several questions noted as to sources beyond our college library, and, alongside my title—"Chaucer's *Parlement of Foules* as a Religious Protest"—she had written "Fascinating!" She asked each of us why we chose our topic. I answered that I saw Chaucer's figures as double images like double exposures on snapshots. I wanted to understand why. Mrs. Adair immediately found the idea intriguing.

The research came naturally and would be much easier than the writing of the Project. Right from the start, I could match some of the mental pictures in the *Parlement of Foules*. Those afternoons of reading I had done with that wonderful "gift of time" were a ready-made index of topics to highlight the path ahead.

First, I want to tell you what I discovered in the research, then acquaint you with the story, and, finally, we'll look at the reactions. The following four topics are reflected in the images of the *Parlement:* Augustine, allegory, cathedrals, and the University of Paris.

Augustine's name came up so frequently in my afternoon readings that I finally had to devote a special search just to him. Augustine, this Bishop of Hippo in North Africa, wrote a great deal, including his well-known *Confessions* and *The City of God.* While his "voice" pervaded religious thought in the fourteenth century, he had died almost 1000 years before (430 A.D.). After his death, his writings remained alive and influential. Only the Bible had more readers in the Middle Ages than Augustine. Both Wyclif and Luther, for example, drew upon his thoughts, as churchmen still do today. An oft-quoted recommendation of Augustine's is that a Christian writer must *teach, delight,* and *move.* Chaucer knew Augustine well. He quotes him as often as he does St. Paul.

Secondly, *Allegory* by Angus Fletcher gives a dynamic description of many aspects of the form, but only two techniques need explanation here. First, an action or word that is odd, unexpected, or inappropriate is a signal for the reader: *Pay attention!* Secondly, Fletcher describes how the hidden intention can be the reverse of how the surface reads. When the levels of an allegory have widely contrasting tones, the contrast gives greater protection to the author, who is expressing sentiments that hostile authority would condemn. While diverse meanings may appear to be simple entertainment, Fletcher calls the various levels a "power struggle." I find that exciting. Skillful concealment is equal to a cloak of invisibility for the author.

Cathedrals, the third topic, with their numberless carvings of leaves and flowers, were often described as gardens that never change. And, though similar elements are found in all—splendid portals, magnificent stained glass windows, awesome interiors—each building is unique. Each reflects the heritage, and the history of its locale. English cathedrals, with their strong horizontal lines and many narrow windows, are recognizably different from those of France. The French, characteristically, have splendid rose windows and a great deal of glass in the outer walls. Italy used its abundance of marble to create patterns of it in various colors on both the exterior and interior. And, within each country, individual cities strove to raise a building that would be better, greater, unlike any other.

The last topic is the University of Paris. It wielded power and influence unequaled by any other school in Europe. Thomas Aquinas, the famous theologian, had taught in Paris. His teachings, and issues of rival philosophies that were divisive in the fourteenth century, were heated topics of debate.

For my study, several books recommended by Mrs. Adair were accessed through Interlibrary Loan. Every week I'd talk with Dr. Ware to report my progress or problems. He thought the religious aspect unusual in Chaucer, but would not object in a Senior Project. (For a doctoral thesis, he assured me, he would have been much more rigorous.) I said Chaucer delved into matters of faith more often than he realized, adding that the Host in the *Canterbury Tales*, for instance, is Christ. My statement did not surprise him, but he didn't agree. On the contrary, "Of course *you* would think that," he said, "because you are a Catholic." Chaucer's also being a Catholic did not seem a consideration.

I complained, somewhat absurdly, that I suffered from the Semmelweis Syndrome. I knew something important but no one would listen to me. (Ignaz Semmelweis had found the cause of childbed fever—germs transmitted between patients by doctor's unwashed hands—but the medical profession ignored his insight.) Dr. Ware found the term creative, but would not acknowledge the possibility.

Numerous activities filled my senior year. Then, suddenly, it was over. Classes were over. The excitement of the Senior Project was over. The family, including my first grandchild, cheered as I got my diploma. After the ceremony, Dr. Ware congratulated me and asked me to stop in at his office during the summer. I found the request odd, but in the midst of family revelry, I gave it no serious thought.

Several weeks went by before I visited the English Department. Dr. Ware had gone on vacation but his secretary had an envelope for me—a bulging envelope. It contained a personal, six-page letter from Dr. Ware. Here is how it began:

> June 21, 1972
> Dear Mrs. Cullen:
> The final draft is much more readable than the last rough that I saw. Your prose is often flat, but at least most of the kinks in the rough draft have been straightened out and the result is a serviceable style.
>
> Your extraordinary bibliography and notes show how diligent you have been in your research; as I mentioned several times during the course of your research, your scholarly zeal is both rare and admirable. Your pursuit of hidden meanings in Chaucer has helped you to acquire a liberal education far more extensive than anything envisioned by the inventors of our Senior Project requirement. You know your way around the library—at least when looking for information about medieval topics—better than many professors. The experience of researching and writing your thesis, in other words, has been a valuable end in itself.
>
> I wish I could congratulate you for having succeeded in all ways, but I cannot. I shall try to dissuade you from your reading of the *Parlement*.

Five pages of *dissuasion* followed, and he closed with, "Sincerely, James M. Ware."

A glance at the first page told me I'd better deal with the remainder in a quiet place at home after dinner. To prepare you to understand the letter, let me give you an idea of the plot of the *Parlement*.

As it begins, Chaucer has been reading an old book, then falls asleep and dreams. In the dream, a guide comes to show him to the entrance of a garden. The garden is unchanging; the trees and flowers do not lose their freshness; the animals do not age. Chaucer finally comes upon a debate among many birds in the presence of Nature herself. The question centers on finding the right mate for a beautiful eagle but reaches no conclusion. The birds elect to return in a year to try again.

The subtitle I had given Mrs. Adair is "a religious protest." If Chaucer planned to express controversial opinions, he would *have* to do it covertly, by his own brand of trickery—and he does. The Guide is nameless, referred to only as "African." Knowing Augustine's centuries of authority, he might as well be a given, but Chaucer slyly conceals the figure's identity. At the outset an African (named Scipio) is introduced. Later, when the Guide arrives he is "in the same array," he's wearing the clothes Scipio had worn. Why draw attention to the clothes? And why not say his name? These are signals that the unnamed African guide is not what he appears. Chaucer confirms the "African" as Augustine when the Guide *instructs* the poet, *comforts* him, and, then, surprisingly, *shoves* him through a gate into a beautiful garden. That's Augustine's *teach, delight,* and, *move*. The "shove" surely catches our attention.

Then there is the matter of the setting of the poem, the location of this *Parlement*. Let's consider the University of Paris, and the many debates. There were those—the reformer Wyclif and others—who found the religious discussions repetitious, even *foolish*. Chaucer, in the midst of the *Parlement,* interjects the complaint, "a *fool* cannot be still." With a cast of talkative birds, Chaucer could have called his poem the Parlement of *Birds*. But he chose instead (thanks to the flexibility of medieval spelling) a title of *two* possibilities: the *Parlement of Fowls* or *of Fools*. Birds chattering on the primary level, can conceal *fools* jabbering as the hidden intent. (I'm quite sure the three prominent birds can be identified as particular theologians by the opinion each expresses.)

And, last is the site of the unchanging garden. Notre Dame Cathedral of Paris made up part of the community of the University of Paris. Many clues to features of the building can be identified as the narrator strolls about the "garden." His ultimate destination is a specific portal *alive* with little birds carved in the stone, the design dominated by a large central statue of a woman—not unlike a figure of Nature herself.

All of these ideas were incorporated into the Senior Project. I had made the acquaintance of several hundred books and journals. One hundred are included in my bibliography. (Sources for the *Parlement* hold valuable information concerning the *Canterbury Tales*, my ultimate aim.) I had also organized 130 pages of information and set it down on paper. My lack of skill as a writer—and hope for the future—reminds me of the first pie I had ever baked. Ted and I managed to break open the crust and eat the apples. But, with patience and repetition, today I can say I bake a terrific apple pie. It just took practice and determination.

Now, to the content of Dr. Ware's letter. His complaints could be valuable for a revision, although not his intention. He observes: "It is clear that parts of the poem, especially toward the beginning, seem to be lost on us modern readers." Fletcher, in his book *Allegory*, points out that unless the reader shares sufficient background with the author, the text may be entertaining, but the depth of its references will hold no meaning.

Professor Ware feels that Augustine was concerned with "pagan contaminations of Christian worship in a way that few men in Chaucer's day were." The opposite, however, is true. Protests were often voiced against lavish celebrations, opulent churches, and Mary's growing dominance. The great number of French churches dedicated to Notre Dame provides concrete evidence of that trend of exaggeration.

And later, although Dr. Ware had seen "moderns" as *dis*advantaged, he now feels we are more knowledgeable. "It is possible, in other words that Chaucer has concerned himself with the origins of Christian practices that smack of paganism—even though he would not have the historical awareness of a modern." It is Chaucer who has the advantage of "awareness." He lived in the midst of developing "pagan" elements. It is *we* who have learned by research. He *knew;* we needed to *discover.*

The professor continues, "The tone and atmosphere of the literal meaning of the poem are completely at odds with the tone and atmosphere of the allegorical meaning you find." That, for him, made my reading, "unconvincing." Hardly the basis of an objection, this divergence proves the creativity of genius. It is the protection by contrast mentioned earlier—the weaving of a cloak of invisibility for the poet.

Finally, challenging the uniqueness I claim for the setting, he asks, "How many of the features of Notre Dame that you discuss would be found in many or most Gothic cathedrals?" Features are necessarily standard, but they are designed individually. Even the interior columns differ from one building to the next. And, in a book that amounts to the biography of the cathedral at Paris, Allan Temko describes birds—some with heads of monks—hopping among the foliage of a portal where there is a central figure of a woman, who could portray Nature.

If the presence of birds surrounding a woman were not a clear enough identifier, we are given one more. Dr. Ware notices that clue. "Once inside it we see the cathedral on a walled island. Has Chaucer simply forgotten his points of reference as he has gone along?" Rather than "forgotten," this is a *specific clue*. Chaucer made me understand that Notre Dame of Paris is *on an island* before I'd ever seen a photograph! That's the clincher. It is, indeed, a "garden" surrounded by a wall in the middle of a river—the River Seine.

All his "dissuasions" made me feel I had not done a proper job. He did not, however, change my mind about what I see in Chaucer's poem.

After sharing the letter with my husband, it didn't take much to convince me to give Chaucer a rest. Ted and I would relax and enjoy the good life. Claremont's good life included a music festival each July. We always had tickets for the entire series of concerts. And, fortunately, so did Mrs. Adair. Just as I entered the hall on the first evening, I heard, "Mrs. Cullen, how are you?" It was Mrs. Adair. She immediately inquired about the Senior Project. I told her how exciting it had been, and then about the sincerely discouraging letter. She asked to read what I'd written, and I delivered the Project to her at the next concert we attended.

Just after eight o'clock the following morning, the phone rang. "Good morning. This is Virginia Adair. I hope I haven't called too early."

I assured her she hadn't.

"I started reading your Project when I got home last night. I couldn't put it down. It's the most original thing I've seen in years. Could you come to my home? We must talk."

We agreed on two that afternoon. She had understood! A Chaucer relationship between us began that day—an essential, life-giving relationship.

Mrs. Adair lived in a large, two-story Spanish Colonial style home in the center of Claremont. A grand avocado tree shaded most of the backyard. I arrived just at two. After a warm welcome, she led me into the high-ceilinged living room. She poured iced tea for us, and then began leafing through the pages of my Project as she commented on what we both knew. "The writing style needs improvement, but," she encouraged, "you'll acquire that with practice. The ideas are the important thing." Then she came to the point, "You must get a Ph.D."

Without a moment's hesitation I said, "No. I have no interest in doing so." I knew graduate students were expected to be "disciples." My personal interests would need to be on hold. To spend an unpredictable number of years in such a program would never enter my head.

Not a woman to dwell on negative thoughts, she switched immediately to Plan B. "Well, then, you need to get published. Begin writing articles. When your name is seen in print frequently enough, they will have to respect you."

That sounded like a fine idea. Many situations in the *Canterbury Tales* have a clever little twist concealed. Organizing clear, succinct explications would give me the practice I needed. We chatted a while about potential subjects. Then, I thanked her for her time and interest and got up to leave.

When we reached the door, she asked my plans for the summer. "The only thing certain," I said, "is celebrating our twenty-fifth wedding anniversary." She congratulated me and we promised to stay in touch.

Ted and I planned to renew our marriage vows at church the morning of August 9, 1972, and have our favorite dinner—lasagna—with the family that night. So much for plans. The lasagna sauce went into the freezer. And the priest we arranged to see at church came to see *me* in the hospital. With the dramatic onset of a problem the evening of August 8, Ted whisked me off to the ER. Dr. Gridley, the new man on the staff, turned out to be a medical hero. Even though I had no pain, he recognized symptoms of a bowel obstruction. The OR and ICU followed. Wonders of modern medicine took precedence over our planned celebration.

Back home two weeks later, having more people wait on me than I ever had in the past, I found the opportunity to write down a portentous "dream" I'd had while under the anesthetic. Mrs. Adair and I were traveling in an old western stagecoach. Though incongruous, we were talking about future Chaucer plans. We agreed to tell the story of the Host first, then the story of Chaucer, and finally the story of all the other Pilgrims. End of dream. When I recounted the dream to her, some weeks later, she said that that would, indeed, be a proper plan. Now I only needed to have a sufficient number of articles accepted to build a reputation.

After that unforeseen hospital sojourn, I began to keep a journal. This entry is self-explanatory:

> I feel each life has a purpose. The strange and intriguing thoughts that have come bursting in on me ever since I began to read Chaucer cannot, I am convinced, be of no value and cannot have no purpose. Having had it forcefully demonstrated to me last month, I know that one can very easily, and with little or no warning, die. I am

determined to work as quickly (but carefully) as possible to get my unorthodox ideas accepted. Unfortunately, there is a large stumbling block I had not anticipated. Because I write poorly, I feel like an intellectual bottleneck: all these marvelous ideas are burgeoning in my brain but my ability to express them seems "clogged."

The journal would act as a vicarious means of sharing my Chaucer thoughts.

I began writing little expositions to submit. Because I wanted as many in print as possible, and soon, I worked on three simultaneously. Two needed only a page or two as a submission. The third, about bees, had to incorporate beekeeping information for the modern reader who knows little or nothing of hives and honey gathering.

First, I sent out a suitably risqué explanation of the *Tale of Sir Thopas*. The almost universal opinion of that story is that it is dull as a laundry list. This view, however, can only be maintained by turning a blind eye to the dominant activity of *pricking* and *being in the saddle*. Yes, the words meant then what they mean now. I crammed as much evidence as I could into the one-page limit. It got a *yes* on first try. Thopas found a life of his own in *The Explicator* for January of 1974. (A reference to that little item is found in the notes for the *Tale of Sir Thopas* in the *Riverside Chaucer*, today's standard college Chaucer text.)

Next came the well-known story of Chaunticleer, the rooster, who is beset with bad dreams. His wife offers an effective remedy, "taak som laxatyf." A form of augury—telling the future by examining the condition of bird's entrails—is concealed in her recommendation. (That piece eventually appeared in *The Explicator*, Fall 1979.)

A third article involved Chaucer's "Litel Jape" (little joke). The Pilgrim Cook says he'll tell a little joke about a misbehaving apprentice—not a *cook's* apprentice, but, significantly, a *food gatherer*. Ambiguous words encourage the second identity of a *bee*, who is "brown as a berry" (perhaps the size of a berry?) and like a "hive full of honey." He is not a worker, but a thieving drone. Fourteenth-century folk knew the habits of bees, because honey had long been the main source of sweetening. After six rejections—with no complaint at all about my writing—I withdrew it from making the rounds for two reasons. First, I had much more to say than allowed by journal limitations.

Second, and more important, as one editor put it, the "ingenuity of [my] argument," impressed him but, ingenuity aside, "the tale makes perfect sense read as a literal tale." A *second level of meaning* held no interest. Clearly, because the story is only read as referring to a wayward adolescent, Chaucer has put one over on us for centuries!

While working on the three articles, I gave a copy of each to Dr. Ware, in hopes that he would see that I was really on to something. He found Thopas "readable" though "it lacks sparkle." He wished me "Good luck" and said *The Explicator* might accept it, which it did. Regarding another story, he closed with, "I realize that most of my comments have been critical rather than complimentary: it takes a lot of argument, not just an appeal to authority, to persuade you to give up your working hypothesis." When he read the Chaunticleer piece, his reply ended with, "Moral: keep your anchor on the hard bottom of literal meanings. Otherwise you'll drift onto the rocks of allegorical nonsense. Cheers, Jim Ware." I no longer saw the point in continuing to try to convince him—or him to try to convince me. Only trivial conversation passed between us after that.

A fourth and larger article had to do with the Host and became a far-reaching endeavor. This explanation had to be thorough and painstaking. I photocopied every entry in the *Canterbury Tales* that includes the Host: his description, the words he utters, the words addressed to him, or said about him. Arranged in sequence, it was like a running conversation. They were no longer scattered fragments, but connecting lines that built a solid portrait, each line strengthening and clarifying the image.

Collecting these lines into one "document" gave a more sharply delineated portrait than I'd seen before. This prompted a number of questions, such as: What is concealed in his cryptic comment concerned with "substance"? Or why does the Pardoner single him out regarding sin? There were many more questions, which made the task appear endless—and exciting. I'd deal with matters of publication when I finished.

Only one brief note had been published to this date. I mulled over the difficulties of getting into print. Although I liked the freedom of following discovery trails on my own, additional course work held an advantage. Familiarity with the basic books and authors of a graduate program would definitely prove useful. It would also give me a greater sense of personal confidence, and, I would hope, it might be the basis of future scholarly relationships. A Master's Degree had all this potential.

I called for an appointment with a Continuing Education counselor at the Claremont Colleges. Though I don't recall her name, the white-haired lady's background is memorable. Many years before, she had been a student of Edith Rickert, a name renowned in the world of Chaucer studies. The poet, predictably, became a lively topic of our conversation. Obviously enthused, she asked how much time I'd spent in England. When I responded that I'd never been there, her well of enthusiasm dried up immediately. "Nothing *new* associated with Chaucer is worthwhile except if it comes from the source, from England."

I told her I found "the source" in Chaucer's words that hold secrets yet to be discovered. That possibility eluded her. Although this counselor proved less than helpful, with Ted's encouragement, I enrolled in the Master's Program at Cal Poly in 1974 with high hopes.

Eager to be going to school again, this time I'd center on the Middle Ages. It would open a new window into Chaucer's world. I took courses in medieval literature beyond the *Canterbury Tales* with Dr. Elliott. He was, after all, the medievalist in the English Department. In addition, directed reading that dealt with heresy and witchcraft, and a general survey from the Philosophy Department were possible. A specialist in the School of Architecture knew Gothic cathedrals, many of which Chaucer could have seen being built. I studied medieval games with the Physical Education Department, and did a survey of illuminated manuscripts with the Art Department.

Still researching Chaucer's Host, with his hidden identity of Christ and therefore the Eucharistic Host, I had to be certain of the date of the establishment of the dogma. I would ask Father Frank Meskill, Chaplain of the Claremont Colleges. The information I wanted whetted his curiosity. When I said it had to do with the *Canterbury Tales*, his eyes lit up. He loved Chaucer. And how did the Eucharistic dogma fit into Chaucer's tales? Because of questions I had about the Canterbury Host, I said Chaucer may have been a heretic. The poor man's face turned purple as he blurted, "He was devout…devout!" I agreed, with reservations. Even then I took Chaucer to be a man of deep faith, though I had questions regarding his attitude toward the Church. Our chat ended abruptly. I never heard from Father Meskill.

Figuring there might be no reply, I went to the Honnold Library at the Claremont Colleges on my own. (Honnold is closer to home than Cal Poly. I used it regularly and with good success.) While muddling along false trails, I had the good fortune to discover reference works I'd never seen before. Checking the card catalog under *Eucharist*, *Church history* and such, I zeroed in on the answer. The Host as the Body of Christ, a tradition which began with the Last Supper, developed as an official dogma in the 1200s. *Corpus Christi*, the feast commemorating the dogma, came to great prominence within Chaucer's lifetime, and was lavishly celebrated. There is no doubt that the *Host* meant *Christ* to Chaucer's contemporaries.

All the work I had done regarding the Host prepared me to respond to a "Call for Papers" posted on the English Department bulletin board, in the spring of 1975. The papers were to be read at the regional meeting of The Conference on Christianity and Literature in January of the next year. Deadline for entries—October 1, 1975. What better setting for announcing the discovery of Christ in the *Canterbury Tales*? I mailed the requested abstract. Imagine my thrill when a letter of acceptance arrived!

What an opportunity! I asked Dr. Richards of the Philosophy Department, who had guided my independent study, if he would read over the Host paper. Not being from the English Department, he would have a different point of view. He returned the paper with this brief comment. "A medieval studies organization would certainly be interested in this paper. You argue a strong case for your conclusion. R. C. Richards." It would be several months before I read the paper. His encouraging words gave me confidence in my approach.

Meanwhile, in my regular class work, Dr. Elliott had assigned a paper for the course that covered Chaucer's works other than the *Canterbury Tales*. I could see a complicated story hidden within Chaucer's *Troilus and Criseyde*. The problem with the research for the subject is that I would need a thorough knowledge of astronomy and astrology. Yes, many books on both subjects are available. Yes, I could talk to astronomers and astrologers. There is the rub. All information, to be valid for my purposes, had to predate 1400! The universe and the forces at work were seen completely differently then. I discovered much arcane data recorded in charts, tables, and cryptic notations. It would be impossible, nevertheless, to be able to use it with expertise and accuracy. So, I chose to learn what I could, and point out possibilities. In that way, I could cross *Troilus and Criseyde* off my mental list of Chaucer's works I would examine.

Mythical figures are important to the story. So is the repetitive vocabulary—ascend, descend, degree, array, as examples—with its alternate celestial connotations. Two "houses" dominate the setting. It is recognized elsewhere (in *The Complaint of Mars*) that Chaucer parallels movements in the heavens with actions of the plot. This happens with the characters in *Troilus* also—that, and much more. Fletcher in his book on allegory, describes religious allegory where action is determined by doctrine. Chaucer, using similar determination, has action correspond to celestial activity. A clever example is the portrayal of an eclipse where a woman that I identify with the moon first gives her glove, then her sleeve to a sun figure. A solstice is also dramatized as the sun figure's face turns red; he stops in the midst of conversing; seems to doze a while, and then awakens.

I begin the paper with the claim that "an atmosphere of astrology and mythology fills the pages of *Troilus and Criseyde.*" My conclusion proposes that "each image may play a role determined by celestial forces, the plot advancing not by the poet's fancy but by his perusal and imaginative use of astronomical tables and astrological charts." I had discovered what I wanted to know related to *Troilus* and, now, could confidently leave the subject as beyond my capabilities—in time and in scholarly attainments.

Dr. Elliott recognized the depth and breadth of my investigation. Even so, he said I "fundamentally misunderstand the nature of medieval allegory." The paper got a barely passing grade.

With that course completed, I gave more time to preparing the paper for the upcoming conference. Chaucer deserved the best possible impression I could make in my maiden appearance before the world of academe. I worked on content, vocabulary, and reading it aloud.

Mrs. Adair asked if I had read the paper before an audience? When I said I had not, she invited me to rehearse my presentation in front of a small group at her home. They gave suggestions about eye contact with the audience, what to emphasize, and which words needed to be pronounced more distinctly. I appreciated that help, but the "best" was yet to come. When I finished the reading, they asked questions! I had to defend what I had said—an invaluable experience. Without it, I'm not sure I could have handled the "pop quiz" that came from the roomful of academics at the conference.

The event took place at the Santa Barbara, California campus of Westmont College in January 1976. Luncheon attendees sat at tables with others from their college or university. Professor Elliott, who would also be reading a paper, sat across the table from me. He said little, and excused himself before the dessert.

I would speak second on a program that began at 2 P.M. The listeners, about thirty of them, were professors from many schools. I began by introducing myself as a student, not one of "them." At the conclusion, three of the professors asked questions. My replies seemed to please the questioners, and my confidence in responding pleased *me*.

I relayed news of the conference to Mrs. Adair at my next visit, and thanked her again for providing my preparation. She asked if anyone had offered to publish my paper, and expressed surprise that no one had. She suggested I incorporate material from the question period and send the revised paper off to the *Christian Scholar's Review*, the journal published by the conference sponsors. I said I would as soon as I caught up with my class work. Now, at mid-quarter, many assignments needed my undivided attention.

In the meantime, a few weeks after the Westmont adventure, a letter came from Professor Carol Jennings, whose talk preceded mine at that afternoon session. She said she wished there had been time to congratulate me on my "fine paper," and continued, "Certainly, it was the most fluent, persuasive, and interesting of all the papers which I listened to during the conference, guest speakers not excepted." She asked for a copy of the paper. Her kind words meant a lot to me, and I wrote promising to honor her request as soon as I had finished the revision.

A few weeks later I mailed the revised version to her and to the *Christian Scholar's Review*. A letter arrived from the *Review* in April to say they had received the paper and would circulate it among their referees, the professors who would decide if the content suited their journal. That decision could take two or three months.

I pushed thoughts of the submission to the back of my mind. The paper would have to take care of itself. Now in my final quarter at Cal Poly there were many projects still to complete, including the oral exam. Ted and I went out for a Mexican dinner when I passed the oral. The end was in sight.

In June 1976, for the auspicious occasion—reception of a Master of Arts degree—my mother came from Chicago. The rest of the family, including four grandchildren, also attended. The little ones were distracted by all the goings-on, but when the rest of the family cheered, so did they as I crossed the stage to receive my diploma.

After graduation, my mother and I spent a week shopping, lunching out, and enjoying the precious new generation. After she left, I cleaned house and tried to catch up with all the tasks that had been put off because school work came first. When my surroundings were in relative order, I gave some thought to "what happens now?"

A letter arrived from Dr. Butterworth, one of my favorite professors, a man of considerable charm and wit, whose judgment I valued. Several months before I had asked him to look over my latest version of the little joke, the bee story. As I suspected, my bee paper had been buried on his desk beneath more pressing matters. It resurfaced as he prepared to leave for the summer.

His note began with a quip, a *bee* reference to himself as one of the "3 bees" in the English department (Bellman, Butterworth, and Bobb), a perennial joke. He also closed with humor. In between, however, he said, "I appreciate your note and the sharing of your investigation with me. Your argument sounds persuasive but I hate allegory." *I hate allegory?* I found that disconcerting. Can you picture a medical doctor stating I hate writing prescriptions? Aren't prescriptions—or allegories—just part of the job? A well-known reference book, *Literature of the Middle Ages,* says that allegory, with its two or three levels of meaning, is what separates the great medieval literature from the mediocre. Surely, no one doubts that Chaucer's writings are great. Then shouldn't we expect to be concerned with allegory? If not, why not?

With Dr. Elliott ruling out allegory in Chaucer, and Dr. Ware referring to allegorical "nonsense," and now Dr. Butterworth hating it, I felt as if—after learning of a legitimate trail—I had been told, "You dare not go there!" In the midst of my confusion, I remembered a supposedly "perfect" book I had received as a gift, *A Preface to Chaucer.* The table of contents, fittingly, includes a chapter on allegory. A quote from the first page of that chapter (p. 286) appalled me. It asserts that today "allegory is almost universally regarded with suspicion, if not with contempt." If this is the common attitude—and in my experience, it surely had been—then the intriguing images I see or want to describe would "universally" evoke suspicion and contempt. What could I do to counteract this attitude? Did I have the ability to make my case? The questions became a tangle in my mind. I could peer at the Pilgrim images but had no skill for unraveling their identities. A visit with Mrs. Adair would be my only help. When the reply came from *Christian Scholar's Review*, I'd make an appointment to see her during her office hour. She and I could talk about the Host paper, and about her feelings—as a poet—in regard to allegory.

The first week of August, the *Review's* long-awaited response arrived. The editor's accompanying letter said, "I am sorry to report that we have decided against publication." He enclosed thoughts from several referees, which I took as a well-meaning gesture on his part.

To help you understand, here is the final summarizing paragraph of my paper that asserts Chaucer's Host conceals the image of Christ.

> Various explanations have previously been given for the problems raised here: the immediate acquiescence of the Pilgrims to the plan of the Host, the variations in the Host's attitude toward each traveler, the meaning of the Host's judgments, the reason that the Host is the one most covered with sin, his singular oaths and unique Latin phrases. If from Chaucer's words we make the assumption that the host is Christ, this fact alone explains them all. Then these, and perhaps many other things, take on a new level of meaning.

A reviewer wrote alongside the paragraph: "A strong claim to make. If true, your paper should be lengthened and these points explicated."

After that first opinion, I wondered, just for a moment, if the others would agree. Perhaps the rejection anticipated a re-submission with additional supportive material.

The introduction to the second critique gave me a fleeting moment of optimism. "If the reading of the *Canterbury Tales* suggested in this paper were to be accepted, the result would be a revolution in Chaucer studies." But, then the reader took me to task because, "the paper ignores the first definition of words in order to choose the third or fourth which better supports its thesis." I asked myself why it should be expected to limit interpretations to first definitions? And what if more than one definition gives a proper reading to a line?

I turned to the third review, now, with growing misgivings:

> This is the kind of thing that will set Christian scholarship back ten years rather than advancing it even a hair. She excuses the Host's profanity with the claim that these are Christ's claims to his sacrificial death, but does anyone actually suppose that our Lord was blasphemous and profane? His references to His own sacrificial death were never made in language which broke the commandment about taking the Lord's name in vain. Naturally, the *Canterbury Tales* is a thoroughly Christian work; but this business of seeing Christ figures everywhere is the "bag" of a secular critic who really doesn't understand anything about Christ.

I read in disbelief. How can Christ *take God's name in vain?* And the judgmental aspect about "a secular critic" surprised and offended me.

The last of the opinions had only two sentences. It closed with, "The *Christian Scholar's Review* should not touch this with a hundred foot pole." My fledgling self-confidence, like a fallen nestling, had been thoroughly trodden on. At that moment, I didn't see how it could survive.

Only a few weeks later, just as the school year began in September, I heard that Mrs. Adair had not returned to teach. In an early morning phone call my friend Lois, a senior at Cal Poly, reported that other faculty members were taking over her classes. And, Lois understood, Mrs. Adair had chosen to retire and would move to the desert, to Shiloh, a place dear to her and her late husband. With that added bit of news, an inertia set in that I found difficult to overcome.

I spent the rest of that day in a pit of frustration searching for a way out. I had a long, serious talk with myself. Before Cal Poly I kept busy with a lot of things, I told myself. I could certainly take up those same interests again. I'm still the same person I was before I took all those college classes—but there my inner voice faltered. I was *not* the same person. Amazing, indelible things had happened to me. Could I just ignore them? Who would care—besides me?

No conclusion forthcoming, the best I could offer myself was to plunge into my former activities with gusto. I would try to restrict all Chaucer plans and expectations to an enclosure, a realm of possibility with little likelihood of probability. It was the fall of 1976.

A ten-year interlude, a time of uncertainty and testing, followed. What I'd naïvely, optimistically taken to be the beginning of a grand adventure—the "special thing" I would do in my life—now became an effort to confine those special thoughts and to provide an enclosure for the protection of my fledgling spirit. I would exist in a haze of Chaucer deprivation. I will admit, however, I had a sense of the poet waiting somewhere beyond that haze.

An occasional question, for example, would nag for an answer: If the Summoner is so very *unsightly*, why is he said to be *attractive to young women*? If Chaucer knew astrology, why does he make such an *apparently* blatant error regarding the exaltation of the moon? I'd jot down the questions, and slip them into a Chaucer repository—a cigar box dedicated to this purpose.

As fall turned to winter, I busied myself with holiday gift projects. When Ted or my children would ask if I planned to do anything more with Chaucer, my standard reply would be—I don't know. I didn't tell them about the cigar box.

Being an incorrigible looker-upper is what finally made me do something of an about-face. My *need* for answers eventually became greater than my *distress* over the attitude of the critics.

The wonder of it refused to be ignored. Christmas 1976 came and went. All the dolls and fruitcakes were distributed. The time had come for a new plan.

Ted and I talked. He said, "You're missing out on a lot of excitement if you don't pursue Chaucer."

I countered with, "It all seems to go nowhere."

Then he suggested, "Maybe the ideas were meant *only for you*, for your own enrichment." That was a different thought!

He continued, "I could drive you to Honnold on Thursday morning on my way to my early class at Cal Poly. You could stay all morning—all afternoon, too, if you wanted." He'd made an offer I couldn't refuse.

By the following Thursday I'd dug out some of the questions I'd been saving "just in case." I gathered books by Ovid, Ptolemy, Macrobius, and other writers Chaucer had read, and settled down at a table at Honnold. I went home on the bus about noon, carrying an armful of books that looked promising.

Searching for an answer would always lead me to another question. I still wanted to know *everything* about the fourteenth century. Many scholars compare Chaucer's works with other literary works of his time, but that seemed such a surface endeavor. I had read that, to understand Shakespeare you need to know sixteenth-century heraldry, nautical terms, etiquette, and everything else. Chaucer deserves the same. I searched everything—clothing, medicine, recipes, anything available.

I took every opportunity, for example, to look for pictures of Canterbury Cathedral. (They were not as easy to come by as pictures of French cathedrals.) I had an idea that art work near the shrine of St. Thomas à Becket, in the Cathedral, might have inspired Chaucer regarding the descriptions of the Pilgrims.

During these years of Chaucer restriction, many special opportunities came my way. For example, I had the privilege of making a wedding dress for one of my daughters. Doll-making could be gratifying. I designed and produced many dolls, each one unique. Those years were also blessed with our full complement of eight grandchildren. That meant even more dolls to make for them—and for church fundraisers, as well. Los Angeles Philharmonic season tickets were more than an opportunity for us. They were a "necessity." One Sunday afternoon a month Ted and I drove into Los Angeles for a concert and had a lovely dinner after. And, in 1980, my husband accepted the responsibility of establishing a group for lay Franciscans at our parish. I assisted him by stuffing envelopes, making cake and coffee, and in any other way I could.

An intriguing feature of this interlude of years is "Chaucer nudges," a series of small—but not insignificant—happenings. A gift came from Illinois. Its little cardboard box so pleased me that I've kept it all these years as a memento. The label reads "The Canterbury Shop."

I also began collecting quotations, words that encouraged me in my peculiar Chaucer situation. This is the very first one: "God chose those whom the world considers absurd to shame the wise; he singled out the weak of this world to shame the strong" (1 Cor 1:27). I wrote the verse on an index card and tacked it to the wall above my desk.

Though I kept active, my frustration lingered. When it became unbearable, I'd scribble something to let off steam. The following example is my "report" of an afternoon spent in the presence of the poet himself.

> I was with Master Chaucer this afternoon. He returned from Italy a few days ago. He saw many things that filled his mind & heart with pain. Sad and terrible things are happening. It must be that the Lord will soon come & make an end to this foul world. All the signs are there. He told me of terrors he had seen & heard about. We pray God will not allow such things to come to England.
>
> He is working carefully on his pilgrimage story. It is wonderful to see. His words are heavy with meaning & yet the lines are so cheery that one might never notice unless they will look deeply for what is stored there as a treasure. There are those who will handle his words & never feel their weight.

Enter Chaucer [53]

> He takes these happenings, these truths, & applies his powers to them &—as if by magic—they become creatures of such complexity & variety. From one side we see a simple picture, from another a noble truth &—if we are skillful enough—from the third side a message as if the Lord himself is speaking to mankind.
> It is a wonder to know Master Chaucer, to hear him speak & to see how he weaves his thought into his words.
> —Master Chaucer's humble servant

I refer, there, to the fact that in the late fourteenth century numerous prophecies foretold the imminent end of the world. This scribbling is evidence that my self-imposed hiatus from being immersed in Chaucer actually provided little comfort.

Occasionally I would write a "fan letter" to Chaucer, because I *had* to express my admiration, my exhilaration for his accomplishment. I felt compelled to tell him of my bedazzlement. *"You must have been spellbound by your own ideas. How all the little pieces fit together—it overwhelms me to think of it. Did you have a chart to keep it all straight? Or was your memory so powerful (photographic memory before photographs?) that it all stayed in order and emerged as you needed it?"* I have never ceased to be amazed at the pilgrimage plan.

Years went by, but then events in the summer of 1986 made it difficult to continue to contain my enthusiasm. The confining walls of the enclosure were strained and weakened by a strong nudge provided by Chicago friends who were visiting California. Don and Pauline could spare us only one evening, so they came to dinner. We caught up on news of the city and our growing families. They had moved and were in a new parish, St. Thomas. We recounted differences from St. Alphonsus, the parish our families had belonged to many years before. At the end of the evening, we said our goodbyes. Then, as I returned to the dining room to clear the table, this is what I saw.

The Canterbury Tales

I had been handed a key—emblazoned with *Canterbury Tales*—to open the ten-year-old enclosure! *Astonished* would be putting it mildly. The explanation, however, is very simple. Don and Pauline's new parish of St. Thomas is not "the Apostle," as I had assumed, but "à Becket," the saint martyred in Canterbury Cathedral. Pauline had left a (folded) copy of her church bulletin for my perusal. The haze spontaneously began to dissipate. It would not be long before my self-imposed Chaucer restrictions would be a thing of the past.

III.

Until One Is Committed

JUST A FEW WEEKS LATER, while preparing dinner, I found that I'd forgotten to buy green onions for a special salad. I interrupted the cooking process for a quick trip to the nearby grocery store, hurried in, selected a bunch of onions, and got into the express line. There were only two ahead of me. My thoughts were on what still had to be done for the meal. The first customer completed her transaction and left. The woman just ahead of me was a small wisp of a person with a bandage covering one eye. Not until she spoke to the clerk did I recognize Mrs. Adair.

"Mrs. Adair!" My loud exclamation startled several people, including me. She turned so that the eye not covered could see me.

"Mrs. Cullen!" She smiled. "How very good to see you. Let's step over to the side when you have finished."

Just seeing her again brought a ray of sunshine. I joined her, and we strolled toward the exit as we talked. "I'm surprised and so happy to see you. I understood you had moved to Shiloh."

She couldn't stifle her laugh. "I've heard that rumor before. Only people who've never seen Shiloh would take it seriously. It has never entered the twentieth century. There is no electricity or plumbing." She laughed again. "I'm still in my 'fortress' on Sixth Street, here in Claremont. But life is challenging—as if I have to point out the obvious."

We were outside the store now. She asked, "Is Chaucer still alive and well? I've thought of you often in the midst of my harum-scarum comings and goings."

A grey Honda had moved out of a parking place and stopped alongside us. The driver might be a college student. "Oh, my coach-and-four has arrived. End of *tête-à-tête*. Do drop me a note telling the latest developments. I'm sorry to rush off, but Louie, my trusty *chauffeur*, has a schedule to keep."

I watched as they drove away. I could hardly wait to tell Ted the green onions story.

Our first rainy day of October, I sent her three pages of news and thoughts, condensing critical reaction to the Host paper, skimming over my discouragement, and emphasizing recent events. I reiterated my joy at seeing her, and expressed concern over her evident eye problem, saying I hoped she'd soon recover.

Early in December, I received a Christmas card and note from her. Referring to Chaucer's Host by his given name, Harry, she said, "We'll have to have a chat about poor Harry. The critics were rough, but at least you roused them!" She loved "rousing" people. She assumed I had revised the Host article and wished me a Merry Christmas.

I had, indeed, begun to think about Chaucer projects, but not the Host. Still hoping to get the bee story accepted, I interviewed a local beekeeper, a retired minister. The life cycle of bees is as predictable now as it had been in the Middle Ages. The reverend reassured me about the accuracy of my claims regarding drones and their disruptive activities in the hive. With even greater confidence, thanks to the reverend, I sent the rewrite out before Christmas. A particularly efficient *Explicator* both received and rejected it by the end of January 1987. I filed it safely away and took up other topics.

Each subject, that is, the background for each Pilgrim, is initially quite overwhelming. A previously untapped area of research often demands a great deal of time for absorbing new knowledge. But I found a thought-provoking observation from the late Oscar Romero (who spoke out for human rights). His words put the overall picture in perspective. "We cannot do everything, and there is a sense of liberation in realizing that. This enables us to do something, to do it very well. It may be incomplete, but it is a beginning." Of course! Simply open a door, point a direction, and others will have the sense of achievement as they continue the quest. The burden of an *impossible* task is overcome. One only needs to *begin* the grand process.

In April of 1987, V. A. Kolve, an eminent Chaucer scholar, drew attention to the fact that 600 years before, in April 1387, Chaucer had begun work on the *Canterbury Tales*. How many students have memorized, "Whan that Aprill with his shoures soote"—April's sweet showers? What a special event to celebrate!

Two ways of celebrating occurred to me. First, still conscious of how quickly, and without notice, one's life can end, I asked Ted to set up our open-reel tape recorder so I could spend an afternoon recording ideas about Chaucer. The spoken word goes much more quickly, more efficiently than writing and rewriting. The tape still exists; it never occurred to us, however, that open-reel tape machines would become a thing of the past.

The second way of celebrating would be a new endeavor, as I describe. *"I'm going to search out and record as much material as possible about the Pilgrims. I've never worked on them as a group before."* Thanks to Oscar Romero, the prospect of the task did not overwhelm me. The descriptive portraits and conversational links between the *Tales* were all photocopied and I used the same method I had with the Host—isolating and connecting all that is said regarding the individual personalities. Next came learning facts about constellations from reference books on stars, to see what matched. (You recall that the Pilgrims have double identities, the second identity being a celestial figure. That's the basis of the adventure, the pursuit.) Chaucer often used a prominent star (or stars) in or near a sign of the zodiac as a clue to the figure's physical appearance, activities, or an association with the description.

One amusing case involves the Monk. Chaucer says the Monk loved hunting. From other clues, we know he is the sign of Leo. What better image of a hunter than a lion? The constellation "Hunting Dogs," traditionally illustrated as greyhounds, is above the sign of Leo. It's no surprise, then, that the Monk's dogs are also greyhounds that move as *swift as fowls in flight*. That's Chaucer clue that tells us the dogs are *not earthbound*.

Ted's driving me to Honnold, every week or so, became part of our regular schedule. It felt so right to be searching for answers again, even if I didn't understand why *I* was the one who had all these questions.

Because of regular trips to Honnold, each with an armload of books, Ted suggested it would be "professional" for me, as a researcher, to buy several of the books I often borrowed and toted. So I did. I also joined the Early English Text Society. Based in England, they produce two or more books of medieval texts *in Middle English* each year.

What had begun twelve months before, with the "Canterbury Tales" picture and then the "rediscovering" of Mrs. Adair, renewed my eagerness for the adventure. But sometimes I felt as if I were working under false pretenses, because I had no way to share what I had found.

August 9, 1987 would be our fortieth wedding anniversary. Ted and I planned a splendid picnic at a nearby park, with all the children and grandchildren and our friends. I wrote to Mrs. Adair telling of the new burst of Chaucer activity, and asking if it would be convenient to talk with her in August, sometime after the ninth. I mentioned our anniversary, and I invited her to the picnic.

A postcard soon arrived with her brief, somewhat alarming, reply. "Interested in Chaucer statement. Congratulations on 40th anniversary approaching. Picnic should be delightful. I am recovering from major surgery—not getting about much. Will see you, I hope, in the autumn. Best, Virginia Adair." She had an irrepressible spirit. Certainly recovery would follow.

Toward the end of the summer, while glancing through a gift catalog, this quotation on a note card caught my eye:

> Until one is committed there is hesitancy, the chance to draw back, always ineffectiveness. Concerning all acts of initiative and creation there is one elementary truth the ignorance of which kills countless ideas and splendid plans.
>
> The moment one definitely commits oneself then

Providence does too. All sorts of things occur to help one that would never otherwise have occurred. A whole stream of events issues from the decision raising in one's favor all manner of unforeseen incidents and meetings and material assistance which no one could have dreamt would have come his way. Whatever you can do or dream you can begin it.

    Boldness has Genius, Power & Magic in it.

—Goethe

The words deeply affected me, as I recorded: *"I took it personally. It's time that I committed myself to the task. I guess 'the task' is getting as much as I can figure out set down on paper. When this whole thing began I was 45; next birthday I'll be 60. It's about time to get organized and get to work. I'll try for publication but it won't be essential."* I made Goethe's powerful words my immediate resolve.

    The haze of Chaucer-deprivation no longer existed. The enclosure, that had both restricted and protected the trampled nestling, stood open. As if a phoenix, my revived confidence emerged with this commitment.

    Plainly, the wonder of Chaucer's second meaning refused to be ignored. My journal for 1988 confides *"The excitement of the quest, the treasures I find, the desire to give what I see to others, captivates me."* The "captivation" is in the poet's words—Why such an odd word *there*? A hideous man has a "cherub's" face? He has a buckler (a shield) made of "cake"? I never tired of checking the vocabulary. The *Middle English Dictionary* held countless surprises. It has been, and still is, the reference work I most often use.

    Having filed the bee story away, I put my main effort into Sir Thopas, a story Pilgrim Chaucer tells. I kept trying to improve the article, to pack it with more information than the early Thopas note in *The Explicator*. As I relate, *"I took the Tale apart almost word by word, and in doing so made several amazing discoveries."* Aside from Thopas there is only one other named character, Sir Olifaunt (Sir Elephant). He threatens Thopas. It is not "bodily harm" he intends; he plans to kill Thopas' horse. Since Thopas' main activity to this point has been *pricking*, his pricking days are being threatened. Thopas will no longer be able to *ride*, no more adventures *in the saddle*. Chaucer gives us only one other clue to identify Sir Elephant—the character swears by "Termagaunt." The Middle Ages believed the name belonged to a god of the Arabs. Those two clues are mighty sparse evidence for a search, but Chaucer knew they would be enough. If a threat is made which will end Thopas' ability to "ride," to continue "pricking," a good guess is that venereal disease is the enemy. With that in mind I took a number of books off the shelf at Honnold, books on the history of disease.

Here's my journal account. *"I had gone to the library knowing what I would find, but not knowing what I was looking for."* Selecting *History and Geography of the Most Important Diseases*, I turned the pages slowly, examining everything. When I got to page 135, I saw "*Elephantiasis Arabum*"—the perfect match. Though *Elephantiasis* is generally thought of as enlargement of the lower extremities, a graphic revelation soon followed. *"In another old book,* Anomalies and Curiosities of Medicine, *there he sat. It was a photograph of a victim of the disease. He* had *to sit a good deal of the time. His scrotum was so large he'd need a wheelbarrow to transport it as he walked. Absolutely astounding! I almost let out a whoop!!"* And, in medieval thinking, if the genitals are attacked, the affliction had to have a sexual basis.

I checked numerous medical definitions in the *Middle English Dictionary*. Many had quotes from a book by Chauliac (physician to the pope in Avignon), written in 1363. The book purportedly encompasses "all" medical knowledge at that time. Honnold had the book. A brief perusal demonstrated it had to be part of my library. The Early English Text Society published it, so I ordered my own copy. When it arrived I resolved to read it cover to cover (640 pp.). I did accomplish the task, but not without difficulty. Besides the medical details, you learn how courageous both doctors and patients had to be to either inflict or endure many of the procedures. There were times when I had to close the book to take time off. For example, it gave details of how to deliver a child whose mother had died during labor. Another section spoke of cauterizing wounds where strong men were needed to restrain the patient. Chauliac, with compassion gained through experience, now and then recommended certain procedures not be used on children or the elderly. The possible cure could not justify the certain agony.

Reflecting on the distress of reading Chauliac, I wonder how many students would pursue its contents. And yet, until we know as much as possible of what Chaucer had experienced, or read, or observed, we will be missing ideas or images he incorporates. We will never know everything, but acquiring fourteenth-century knowledge should be an ongoing activity.

I had read a good deal about splendid French cathedrals, and learned how prominent the figure of Notre Dame (Our Lady) had become. Statues in French cathedrals often show a mature, regal woman and Christ, her son, as a tiny child. The French Middle Ages developed plays and stories that distort the image of Mary, the adolescent mother of the Child Jesus. She is portrayed as having heavenly powers to rival those of God Himself. Here is just one example of this exaggeration as described in Jackson's *The Literature of the Middle Ages*. Plays called *Miracles of Our Lady* were very popular in fourteenth-century France. Forty such plays survive. A common thread to each story is that appalling sins were unhesitatingly committed, but a sinner found salvation by the "direct intervention" of the Virgin (pp. 312–14). What a deplorable distortion.

Churches throughout France are dedicated to Our Lady, to Notre Dame. In contrast, the medieval church that is the destination of the Canterbury Pilgrims is named Christchurch. England's main devotion involved Christ's passion and his holy name. Medieval *English* prayers offer a religious feeling different from the church in France. An ordinary prayer asks, "Jesu, for Thy Holy Name,/ And for Thy bitter Passion,/ Save me from sin and shame/ And endless damnation." The straightforwardness of the prayers is refreshing.

Both the medical information I acquired, and understanding the attitude toward Mary, the mother of Jesus, would prove important in considering Thopas. The story can stand on its own, so I devoted a good deal of time to tracing down all the loose ends. I smile, now, when I read my statement about words from the *Tale* that eluded interpretation, that had not yet revealed their secrets. *"The words I cannot decipher are the locations Flaundres (philander didn't work), Poperyng (Pope ring?—but it doesn't go anywhere), and Brugges (complete blank)."* A number of years later—and completely by accident—I found a remarkable answer for each name.

Names, I might add, like those just mentioned, are noteworthy. Chaucer uses names sparingly. I'm certain this is because the choice had to meet so many requirements. As I observe, *"Chaucer, I'm sure, found it difficult to come up with exactly the right name to fit his complex images. When he did find just the right name, it was loaded with meaning—a treasure trove. The possibilities are so exciting. I sure hope I get to share them with someone someday."* I was so eager, and so at a loss.

Late in 1989, a technological event took place at our house. A personal computer came into our lives, my husband's impossible dream come true. His first job out of college had been with IBM, where he learned all about a computer that filled an entire air-conditioned room. (It had to be in air-conditioning because it operated with heat-generating vacuum tubes.) He stayed with IBM for only a few months; his heart really belonged to teaching. Can you imagine his thrill now to have his very own computer on a desk at home—a computer more versatile than the one he learned to use in the 1950s?

The computer benefited me, too, because it is much more forgiving about my abominable typing "skills" than the old Remington I'd been using. But it can also be completely befuddling. I used it as my new typewriter with the understanding that, if I plaintively called, "Honey," Ted would come and fix what had gone wrong.

One day while he did some errands, I decided to type. Soon after I started, the title of the page jumped down into the text. That startled me, but when I tried adding a few words they did appear on the screen. A few more did the same. The title just continued to run ahead of what I typed. I knew Ted would make it right when he got home, so I continued.

When he arrived, Ted approached the machine, and with a few strokes of his special magic, the title took its proper position. It gave no resistance whatever. I never understood. I never asked for an explanation.

When I had the Thopas piece as tight as I could make it, Ted "printed it out" for me (another part of his magic). The computer pages were so clear, and the print so easy to read, they would surely make a better impression than my typed pages ever had. I sent it off on Nov. 6, 1989 to what seemed a receptive journal, *Texas Studies in Literature and Language*. With efficiency to match that of *The Explicator*, the rejection arrived by Dec. 6, 1989. The enclosed review said the research on the vocabulary "is not to be dismissed." They suggested I reduce it to a "glossary of obscenities." Or, it could be revised with "explanation and enlarging the discussion of theoretical function in the *Canterbury Tales*." What a dilemma. It is too long the way it is, *or* even more details should make it longer. When I sent the reviewer's opinion to Mrs. Adair, she—ever enthusiastic—said, "the dismissal was encouraging." And she wished me a Merry Christmas. Since her surgery, we had not seen each other, but kept in touch with occasional notes.

After the holidays, I continued to work on Thopas. There were always new words to check, or a new way to interpret a line. And the persistent question—Did that change the overall picture?

My husband generally read the local newspaper while I made breakfast. He surprised me with a question one morning. "Isn't Thopas the story you're working on?"

"Yes. Why do you ask?"

Ted's reply proved more surprising than his question. "A visiting professor is going to give a lecture on Thopas at Honnold on March 21."

Ted and I went to the lecture, of course. I thought it would be a great opportunity to hear someone at the cutting edge of Chaucer research. It didn't turn out quite that way.

[64] Ensnared by His Words

Here is my reaction to Professor John Alford, the visiting professor from the Midwest, teaching at the University of California at Irvine, and author of a forthcoming book on the *Canterbury Tales*.

The lecturer began with amusing academic anecdotes. When he got around to Chaucer he made quick work of this *Tale of Thopas*, explaining that it's so dull he's sure no one reads it unless it's assigned—and no teacher with concern for students would be likely to assign it. The audience laughed loudly. He gave us his perceptive analysis in a brief demonstration of how the first 10 lines or so follow usual medieval conventions. The remaining 150 lines or more got a token mention as following similar conventions. He finished with more comic material, then on to the wine and cookies.

During the plentiful applause, I tugged at Ted's sleeve and motioned toward the exit. I had no desire for refreshments. I was furious. I didn't want to risk losing my composure altogether. I had just heard the established write-off—it's just "too dull" to bother with. Professor Alford had come to entertain, not to enlighten, as I had hoped.

A few days later, when I had cooled down, I sent the professor a query. He had not mentioned the presence of Sir Elephant. I asked him to explain, if this is the only other character in the story, what purpose does he serve in the plot?

His rather lengthy response arrived a few weeks later. He didn't figure "the meeting with Sir Oliphant fits in at all with the scheme of personal attributes I [that is, Alford] was arguing formed the basis of *Sir Thopas*." The narrator "really had nowhere to go; maybe that's the point…there was no need to continue past the absurdity of 'Sir Oliphant.'" He closed with, "This is probably not an entirely satisfactory answer. But thank you for prodding me to think further about the issue. All best wishes, John A. Alford."

Chaucer's Thopas, to me, held such potential. It needed and deserved to have all the pieces shaken up, the old residue cleaned off, and the pieces put back together. What I saw, what I wrote about, offered a new perspective. Chaucer's words paint a lively, bright, colorful—anything but dull—picture.

I mailed my latest version of Thopas to the *Chaucer Review* a few days after attending the lecture. A postcard from them said they would try to give it "an early read." They were good as their word; the rejection took only six weeks. The critically important definition of "lewednesse" as *lascivious* they considered lacked authority because that sense "was just coming in and would not be the first meaning to occur." Beyond that, they saw one of my medical assertions as unworkable, and another as throwing the "Marian cult into complete disorder." This last objection ran contrary to what I had learned about England's religious thought. Mary, the mother of Jesus, was not the dominant figure in British devotion. Again, the standard interpretation prevailed. I'm seen as side-stepping the obvious meaning of words, or of the story! They didn't understand that I did not intend to destroy the old reading; I offered an *additional new* one. Parallel or dual storylines in Chaucer are not accepted.

The year 1990 brought many changes in our life. Ask any woman whose husband retires. It pleased me that Ted, who had worked hard all his life (sometimes at three jobs), now had blocks of time for his own interests—mainly playing music and writing original computer programs.

I made adjustments in my previous day-to-day schedule, but continued with my research. One of my long, continuing projects aimed at finding detailed pictures of Canterbury Cathedral, in order to check out a theory about possible zodiac illustrations. No adequate pictures had yet come my way.

After gathering much medieval insight about Chaucer's portrayal of the Pilgrims in the *General Prologue*, I created two simple charts on large poster paper. One matched the Pilgrims to their myths and to astrology. The other chart gave me historic facts at a glance in comparison to events of Chaucer's life: What he saw, who he knew, English history, Wyclif, John of Gaunt, the papacy in Rome and Avignon, the Black Death, and the kings the poet served—Edward III, Richard II, and Henry IV. I tacked the charts to the wall where I worked and added details as they came along.

IV.

Write a Book?

With Thopas at a dead end, I returned to work in earnest on the Host. Over the years I'd found a great deal of new evidence to improve that paper I had read at the conference in 1976. Additional material gave me both positive and negative feelings. My journal laments, *"There is a lot more information from many sources. The paper will have a lot more meat, but it will also be more complicated. (GROAN)."* Theology about the Eucharist, images of the festival day of *Corpus Christi*, and comments on the Inquisition, were all vitally important. Could I make all the complexities understandable?

Another matter also bothered me. Because many hidden ideas were religious, would exposing them do harm to the poet's reputation? Actually, the "clues" seemed so obvious to me that I thought there might be a benign conspiracy protecting Chaucer. Would my impressions put him in a bad light? I needed to settle this in my mind before I could forge ahead. I dropped in at the McAlister Center at the Claremont Colleges to talk to Father Brown, the Catholic chaplain on campus. His solution to my hesitancy was simple. His words have guided me ever since: Never fear the truth. No longer "fearful," the time had come to get to work.

Each subject I pursued would provide information about other subjects as well. I scribbled notes to slip into a collection of cigar boxes, each one labeled for an individual Pilgrim. I thought about writing a commentary of some sort, but it seemed pointless. Not only did scholarly journals exhibit little interest, but, with finding more and more material, what I wrote would naturally have to go beyond the page limit. Abiding by page limits would never allow enough evidence to convince anyone of my unorthodox views.

I'm not sure why it took so long to recognize the problem. Perhaps because Mrs. Adair suggested writing "little articles," so my name would frequently be in print. That approach had proven to have flaws. Another reason may have been that, if I had failed to produce an acceptable twelve to fifteen page explication, I didn't see how I would be able to write something longer. In spite of all of that, one day I remembered the original "plan," the one that came to me in that memorable dream where Mrs. Adair and I were riding in a coach. The dream said to tell about the Host first, then about Chaucer, then about all the Pilgrims. There is the answer. *I would write a book.* Its subject would be the Host.

I set about sorting out the notes I'd gathered about the Host, and jotted down questions the book must answer, and additional questions that occurred to me: Why would Chaucer want to hide a meaning, especially a religious meaning? What did the people of the fourteenth century see as the traditional image of Christ? And how can I prove the Host fits that image? I had to have those answers before beginning to write the book. The task would be difficult, but time and persistence would be all I'd need. I was eager for the treasures that would be revealed!

There is great value in time spent thinking and planning before you begin a project. A perfect block of time for thinking presented itself. In May of 1992, my red spiral notebook for jotting down thoughts accompanied me in my carry-on bag for a trip to Illinois to celebrate my mother's eighty-fifth birthday. What a grand weekend! Invitations sent by my brother and sister brought together four generations of our family. Some youngsters I'd never seen except in snapshots. The time flew by.

You will remember that I kept looking for pictures of the Canterbury Cathedral to see the shrine of St. Thomas à Becket. Strangely enough, the end of my search came as a byproduct of that birthday trip. On my way back home to California, a British woman sat next to me. I asked if she happened to be acquainted with the city of Canterbury. She had lived there for forty years! I asked my ongoing question: Can you recommend a book of detailed pictures of the Cathedral? With her charming accent, she replied, "No, but why don't you write to the gift shop at the Cathedral. They have lovely souvenir picture books."

So easy, but I'd never thought of it. The cathedral sent me their catalog, and I purchased a book with precisely the pictures I'd been looking for. Zodiac figures were, indeed, represented at the shrine of Thomas à Becket, but they were *not* arranged as I thought they might be. A search with a positive result gets a celebration. But when the result is negative, it is still a good thing because the subject can be crossed off your mental list. The list just got simpler.

Though I planned to write a book, its time had not yet come. In July of 1992, about six weeks after I returned from the birthday trip, Chaucer quietly sequestered himself in the guest house at the back of my mind. He remained there unstirring, unnoticed for more than a year.

Life is filled with happenings we do not anticipate. Ted, my husband, had been diagnosed with cancer. It proved to be terminal. In a year's time my computer expert, my constant Chaucer supporter, my dearest friend was gone.

Victor, a long-time family friend, had been in Europe when Ted died. Upon his return, several months later, he took me to dinner. As we sat enjoying coffee and dessert, he asked, with obvious concern, "Well, Dolores, what now?"

What a strange question, I thought. I'm sure he could hear the surprise in my voice when I answered, "Chaucer! What else?"

After all the matters that needed taking care of had *been* taken care of, I took a trip back to Illinois for a change of scenery in December 1993. The weather was bitterly cold. My coat and knitted cap and mittens were warm enough, but I thought my face would freeze. Several weeks there, some of the time shopping in the Loop, treading those streets of downtown Chicago that belonged to an earlier time of my life, gave me a sense of a different kind of *me*. I visited the Franciscan church—St. Peter's in the Loop—which had been a formative element of my life nearly fifty years before. A part of me still existed there. It embraced the *me* of now, and supported the woman I had become.

As I left the church, tiny snowflakes floated in the frosty air. Chicago had not yet had its first snowfall of the season. A prelude of flakes swirled on the sidewalk, gusts of wind choreographing them. Anticipation of snow, the promise about to be fulfilled, brought smiles to my fellow pedestrians. As I made my way toward the terminal, when the time of departure drew near, a thin layer of white remained on the walkways. Snow crunched beneath my shoes as it had so many years before. My leaving Chicago and arriving in California would be a kind of reenactment and yet completely different—as my life had recently become completely different.

Prior to my leaving for Illinois, a book catalog had come in the mail. Leafing through it, a title attracted me, *Writing with Power* by Peter Elbow. Publication by Oxford Press recommended the book. I dearly wanted to gain "power" with my writing, so I ordered it. The book lay in the stack of mail waiting for me when I arrived home.

I had set a date for myself—January 1, 1994. That would be the date that my continuing effort—which continues to this day—would begin. It is an effort to retain and revitalize recognition of the genius of Chaucer! And to tell the world about life-changing, literature-changing secrets hidden in the creative words of his *Canterbury Tales*.

Part of my New Year/new life ritual would be to examine the Peter Elbow book. The Table of Contents, and the style of presentation were comfortable, refreshing. My journal entry rejoiced. An image filled my mind. *"I saw myself dancing! Just freely dancing, arms outstretched, free and enjoying the motions. What an amazing sensation!"* The book had already had a positive effect on me. Two recommendations were stressed: Do ten-minute writing exercises every day, and find a group of writers to give you feedback. I affirmed, *"I plan to devote myself wholeheartedly to the directives of Peter Elbow's book."*

My journal often complains that I'm afraid I won't be able

to make my ideas clear, understandable. I saw my writing as stiff, uninteresting. *"I hope the book will get me past some of that."* I confess to being *"frightened"* and feeling *"hopeless."* What I produced could not compare to beautiful prose I had read. *"But,"* I declare, *"in spite of this lack of beautiful prose I have something I want—I need—to say. I can't give it up. I put it off for several years, but I'm not going to put it off again."*

Imagine how much of a kindred spirit I felt with Peter Elbow when I discovered these words in *his* book.

> The reason I finally got myself writing again was my belief that I had something important to say and my decision, in effect, to force the world to listen to me. I didn't just want to get things written for my own pleasure. I didn't just want to hand something in that would satisfy or even dazzle some examiner or judge; I wanted lots of people to believe what I was saying, to change their minds, and damn it, to change their behavior.

He, this recognized author, this academic of repute, had felt what I felt. Downright uncanny. I'm *not* the only one.

With added confidence in the book, I searched out what may have been the only writers' group in Claremont. It met at the senior center on Tuesday mornings. The very next Tuesday I arrived not knowing what to expect. About a dozen, mostly gray-haired folks (like me), were seated around a table in a room with large windows. A moderator, Nelle Fertig, introduced herself to me. Then each person in turn smiled and said their name. Each writer could bring a maximum of two typed pages to read. They generously allowed that I could bring my offerings handwritten, for the time being. The old IBM needed to be restored to action.

It had been a year since anyone had touched the computer. Bill, a man the age of my children and expert with IBM computers, checked it out for me and found it in working order. He reminded me about the process of how to turn it on and turn it off. The term "boot" did not come easily to me. And "switching it off" entailed a step-by-step process—exit this, click that, allowing each command to carry through before signaling the next. Finally, I'd turn off the power. I wrote down the routine, so I'd remember it all. Bill showed me how to direct the continuous-feed paper up and over, so the little pegs matched the holes. We made a space for the catch basket to hold the pages as they'd fold and fall into it. Tearing the pages apart, and removing the perforated edges neatly also took a special skill.

I used the IBM for a week or two—until a box suddenly appeared on the screen advising "ERROR 630 HAS OCCURRED." Bill, by phone, recommended shutting the computer down. A repair person examined the machine and apologetically confessed that the manufacturer no longer made the part that needed to be replaced. Back to hand-written pieces for the writers' group while I tried to figure out what to do.

If I planned to write a book, I'd never manage with a typewriter, not as poorly as I type. Viola, one of the writers, suggested an electric word-processor. She printed each page only after it had her approval. I'd have to think about that.

Two friends, Bob Sorteberg and Judy Wenrick, who both sympathized with my quandary, gave the same advice separately, "You need a Mac." Judy encouraged me to come see a demonstration of hers. It communicated with real words—"Your printer is out of paper"—and it meant *plain sheets of paper*. That, and other friendly features, like choosing "shut down" that handles all the steps to turn the computer off, convinced me.

Bill took me computer-shopping to buy exactly the components Judy had demonstrated. When we brought all the boxes into my house, I told Bill I would take over. I wanted to get to know the Mac. We—the Mac and I—were going to be co-workers. As I recount, *"I unpacked all the hardware—read set-up instructions—and as I went through the user-friendly steps, I simply hooked it all up: printer, mouse, monitor, computer. (My years of experience helping Ted plug in hi-fi connections made it seem natural.) Tomorrow I'll devote myself to the software. For now, I'm going to relax and have a glass of wine with dinner."*

Next day, the Mac, indeed, proved user-friendly. But the printer did not respond. I must say that one of the nicest things about the Mac, problems aside, is that I no longer felt I would *instantly create a disaster* by hitting the wrong key. For example, it might ask, "Do you really want to delete that?" How wonderful to be given a second chance.

To try to solve my printer problem, I started from the beginning, reinstalled everything. When I repeated the steps, cheery words appeared on the screen. "The installation has been successful." In this "must do" situation, I wrote, *"It feels strange to be 'on my own,' one-on-one with a computer, but other sixty-five-year-old women have managed it. I must repeatedly tell myself it's possible."*

Though eager to do a good job for Chaucer, a little voice would taunt me. "What makes you think YOU will be able to do the job?" The necessary answer to that prickly question came from Neil Simon by way of *Christopher News Notes*.

> Playwright Neil Simon says, "Don't listen when the little voice of fear inside you rears its ugly head and says, 'They're taller, blonder, prettier, and they have connections.'" Don't wait for somebody "better equipped." Often the main qualification is just caring enough to take the initiative.

I did admit I had "initiative." I tacked that reminder to my wall.

Late in the spring of 1994, I began scrutinizing each note tucked away in the cigar box labeled "Host." I had the urge to resume looking up words and following their trails to see where they led. And, when I apologized to the writers' group, because my pieces weren't more interesting, they told me they enjoyed my stories about Chaucer. Nelle went so far as to say she couldn't see that I needed her advice. "An academic break is what would be most helpful," she said. What a pat on the back! I figured Professor Elbow's book must be making a difference.

Along about the end of May, I announced that I planned to start seriously working on a book. They all encouraged me and said I'd have all summer for the job, because the group was connected to a school system, and would not meet again until the fall. It's not possible! How can I write for three months without feedback?

Viola, of the word processor, came to my rescue. "Dolores, don't fret. I know where another group of writers meets. If you're free on Wednesday afternoon, I'll take you there."

We met at the bus stop in downtown Claremont and traveled for twenty minutes to an adjoining town, San Dimas. The Civic Center there—one square block—included city hall, a public library, the senior center, and a park. Because I didn't want these new people to get a stuffy first impression of me, I brought a story about my dog. The seven members had much more table space than they needed. All were retirement age, except for one woman in her forties. The San Dimas group offered quite a contrast from Claremont. Claremonters mainly wrote about their lives for their grandchildren, composed letters to the editor, and produced essays expressing opinions on local matters. These folks in San Dimas, on the other hand, were almost all working on books they expected to offer to publishers. They were quite serious and brought ten pages each week.

Viola had been there before, and knew a couple of the people. They gave us a warm greeting. Viola introduced me and, having completed her job as Good Samaritan, now left me on my own. Henry and Art were rewriting their first novels. Henry's, set in Hong Kong, told of a war romance. Art's traversed the centuries with the story of fabled Cain as the Wandering Jew, unable to die. Elaine, a much-published feature columnist, read about her latest project—the history of Burma Shave signs. Linda, the young woman, read an excessively gory chapter from her tale of horror. John, the moderator, who had often made it into print, had us laughing. His stories always closed with a punch line. My small effort got a nice reception. I did add that I generally wrote about Chaucer, but thought it best not to elaborate.

The following week I brought five pages about Chaucer. As I started to read, you could feel a reserved atmosphere in the room.

Write a Book? [75]

When I finished reading, "horror story" Linda blurted, "That was dry as dust!" (I would learn she was prone to blurting.) Elaine and Art immediately asked questions about what I'd read. I think they wanted to demonstrate they had been attentive and were interested in my proclaimed favorite topic.

This group gave me a cultural cross-section—east coast, and west coast, as well as other countries. Henry came from China, Art from Mexico, and Linda had seen the world as a Marine. All the members were happy to help this come-lately novice. I had dealt with journal editors, but book publishers were another breed and I counted on San Dimas' know-how where publishers were concerned.

Several members were Catholic and readily understood what I said about the Host—the central topic of the book. My challenge, of course, would be for explanations so clear that every person knew precisely what I meant. Linda became an unexpected asset when I talked about the Middle Ages not "taking the Lord's name in vain." She had no idea what the phrase meant. So I assumed there would also be readers unfamiliar with the expression. I added one whole page to demonstrate motivation, and included common euphemisms, such as, *egad* and *gadzooks*. Today's *gosh* and *golly* are remnants of that same thinking.

The basic outline of the book had begun as the paper I had read at the conference in 1976. In addition, I had created a short list of questions in 1992, before Ted became ill. The answers to those questions would be woven into the book. I knew my ideas about the hidden identity of the Host would cause the formal Chaucer world to turn upside-down, so I decided on the title "Chaucer's Host: Up-so-doun." (That would be Chaucer's word for *upsidedown*.)

My Honnold library card had expired quite a while back. My next project would be to arrange for a new one. Claremont residents got a break, but I took a check along, not knowing how much the fee for non-students had increased. A young woman at the circulation desk looked at my old card, asked if my address had changed, positioned me to take an ID photo, and filled in some information on her computer screen. As she handed me the new photo ID card, I reminded her I had not yet paid. She smiled and said, "There *is* no charge for senior citizens." What a splendid gesture on the part of the library administration. What an encouragement and sense of value it gave the older people in Claremont. One day I would say a special "Thank you."

Tucking the new card into my wallet, I was now equipped to begin. I would search out the definitions, the connotations, the ambiguities, the evasions and tricks that are Chaucer's forte. My journal says, *"I think it will be quite delicious and amusing."*

First, I dug out the list of questions from my zipper bag, then gathered reference books whose titles I had made note of. I settled down at a big table in Honnold with eight or ten books spread out around me. I was in my element. Hunger cut my visit short and prompted me to take the bus home at noon, carrying an armful of intriguing books. After that first day, if I expected to be gone from home past the lunch hour, I'd take a sandwich to eat on a bench outdoors.

Each answer I searched for would, as usual, beget another question. No telling where it would all lead, but I looked forward to the journey. As I came across a reference with potential, I'd make a tiny note of it, and then another note, and another. I carried these little memos with me, crossing them off as I examined the book involved. I'd either borrow the book to read, or delete it as of no interest. Mostly, I took the books home and read significant portions of them.

My reading often mentioned a book called *Cursor Mundi*. The title means *the course of*, or *the history of*, the world—from creation to the world's end. I looked for it on the library shelf for several weeks, but it never appeared. I finally asked at the circulation desk about the due date of the book, and would they notify me of its return? The clerk found the name of the borrower and told me that one of the professors had checked out the book months ago. Faculty members had no time limit on borrowing. I'm sure she saw my disappointment. She asked me to wait, and made a phone call. Though the professor did not answer his phone, she left a message indicating a "student" had asked about the book. We'd have to wait to see if he chose to return it.

Next afternoon my doorbell rang. A tall man with glasses stood at the door, a large book in his hand. He asked my name. When I identified myself as Dolores Cullen, he handed me the book—*Cursor Mundi*. He explained, "I wanted to see for myself the one *other* person in Claremont who is interested in this book."

I thanked him for his kind gesture, and asked *his* name—Dick Barnes, the professor who taught Chaucer classes at Pomona College, no less. One day I would express my special gratitude to him.

My days were full. I'd spend many hours each week at Honnold. Books I brought home held all sorts of exciting information. For example, illustrations of mythological figures (like Apollo) were transposed to represent Christ; knights and bishops were unquestioningly accepted as part of the cast in plays based on the Bible; and it was believed that the influence of the planet Saturn, at certain times of the day, astrologically, would cause medicine to make a patient ill rather than well. Taking notes, keeping information organized, photocopying memorable sections of the books, and each week preparing eight to ten pages to read to the San Dimas writers kept me busy. Hour after hour brought stimulating surprises.

Most of my time spent at Honnold would find me with my nose in the MED—the *Middle English Dictionary*. Figuring I had nothing to lose, I contacted the dictionary's publisher, the University of Michigan at Ann Arbor. I inquired as to whether I, a person outside the academic community, could subscribe to this dictionary. It had been a work in progress since the 1950s, and this was 1994. The answer? *Yes*. Now, with my own MED, I could stay up late, cozy in my housecoat and slippers, looking for the meaning of Chaucer's words. What more could this researcher want?

V.

Virginia Hamilton Adair

You've seen Mrs. Adair now and then as this story has unfolded. Now we'll zoom in and do a cameo, a feature story, of the part she played in my Chaucer pursuit. Without her, there would have been no pursuit at all.

As the 1994 Christmas holidays approached, with my new life taking shape, I wrote a newsy note to Mrs. Adair. It had been almost two years since we had seen each other. Not until spring of 1995 did I get a reply to my Christmas note, and her envelope had a new return address. Though somewhat surprised, I shouldn't have been. Many things had changed in her life, too. She had left her ten-room, two-story, Spanish Colonial home. Now her days—and nights—were compacted into one room of assisted-living at Pilgrim Place, a retirement village in the center of Claremont. The reason for such a drastic move? Mrs. Adair had lost her sight. What a heavy burden, I thought, for a writer, a poet! My concern that she may have also lost her spunk, her joy of living, vanished as soon as I knocked on the door to her room. My knock immediately brought a cheerful, "Come in."

When I announced, "Mrs. Adair, this is Dolores Cullen," her face lit up. She extended her hand, and I took it. Before I could say another word, she made this pronouncement, "We have to come to an understanding. If you are going to call me 'Mrs. Adair,' I will have to continue to call you 'Mrs. Cullen.' I would much prefer 'Virginia' and 'Dolores.'"

I said, "Of course, Virginia." She couldn't see my smile, but she could hear it. From that moment on, we were no longer professor and student. We were friends.

* * *

[80] Ensnared by His Words

At the very beginning, Virginia, whose professional name is Virginia Hamilton Adair, had been my guide and counselor. She tried in every way she could to recommend me and endorse my Chaucer insight. Had Virginia not believed in me, I would never have told the world about the wonders concealed in Chaucer's words. She had helped me believe in myself—and she continued to do so.

A happy event in her present circumstances, at age 83, her first book of poems would soon be published. A critic likened her to a "comet" that had entered our literary world. Even with all her personal excitement, she made time to hear of my progress and to say a positive word.

When I first knew her at Cal Poly, she had written to me about my senior project, the *Parlement of Foules*. "I am impressed with your scholarship and reasoning in this paper (though I know little of the theology involved)." While others told me I saw things that didn't exist, she had opened a window of sunlit possibility. I need not think only of dark discouragement.

And after I'd had multiple rejections of the bee paper, she suggested we get together for "some tea and sympathy." Our schedules, however, were difficult to coordinate for a visit. To give me something to think about in the meantime, she offered sage advice: "Argue, agree, question—as an equal—but *don't* ask the Big Boys to read your paper, give an opinion or advice unless you're submitting it to an editor for publication. Just sounding off. Don't mean to sound bossy. Best, VHA." I had difficulty feeling "an equal" to these "Big Boys" she referred to. I surely had not been treated as if I were on a par with them, but more about that later.

Though I didn't know about letters of affirmation, Virginia volunteered, "I will be willing to write a letter for you, if ever needed, to affirm your scholarship and good faith."

With the publication of her first book (there would be two more), an article about her and her poetry appeared in *The New Yorker*, December 1995; the title, "Dancing in the Dark." Those are words Virginia used when speaking of her blindness. She became a local news item. The recognition she received pleased me greatly.

I enclosed a note of congratulation in my Christmas card, and told her a bit of personal news. In March she typed the following reply on her Smith-Corona portable, a permanent fixture on her table-of-many-purposes in front of her couch.

```
ᴅear ᴅolores ᵕullen,
     ɪou were so good to write, and ᴊ was delighted to hear from you.
ᵣorgive my ᴅlind staggers on this old portabɪe typewriter; ᴊ can no
longer see the guide keysand most of my writing needs a cryptogr
grapher. ɪ tried to call you nut the only ·ullen was a man who denied
knowledge of you. ɪ have always ᴅeen interested in your .haucer
resear ch projectd, anᴅ hope some time around mid ··arch you will
give me a ring and set up a date to teɪl me about your current
findings or theories. I am  swamped with letters and calls and
still manage to write aᴅout thirty poems a month, a good enough
pastime. ᴅo let me hear from you later in ꞌꞌarch.
     with admiratiomand best wishes,



1 ᴍarch 1996
```

Virginia paints a picture of who she has become—with her blindness and the publication of *Ants on the Melon*. Her closing expressed such confidence in me as I tried to open a door to the publishing world. Signed, with the signature her fingers still remembered, makes her note a treasure.

One day when I veered off the track, Virginia tersely put me back on course. Mainly expressing frustration, I complained, "If someone had *proved* to me a long time ago, that I was wrong, it sure would have saved me a lot of trouble."

Her brow furrowed as she scolded, "That's a foolish statement." She was right, and I knew it.

While I kept plodding along in pursuit of the elusive publisher, life became quite hectic for Virginia, the sudden celebrity.

Translations of her book, TV interviews, the preparation of a second book, all took up a great deal of her time. We saw each other every month or so to keep up with happenings. In mid-1997 I told her a small press had an interest in the Host book, and asked her for permission to dedicate the book to her. Would she be willing to identify herself to the world as approving of my views on Chaucer?

At first she balked, not because she would rather disassociate herself, but because she felt it too great an honor for the part she had played. In our original relationship, with me as her student, she knew only of the "dissuasion" of Dr. Ware. The time had come for her to hear about Dr. Elliott's rejection of Chaucer allegory and Dr. Chorney's "mind your humility." She sat on her couch, cross-legged like a kindergartener, and listened. When I'd get to a professorial rebuff, she would smack her thigh and say, "Damn!" After two of my stories, she recognized how differently she had treated me—and accepted the role of dedicatee.

The Host book, indeed, got published, but I'll talk about my adventure with that a little later. Soon after I had the thrill of receiving my personal copies of the book, I took one as a gift to Virginia. She couldn't have been more overjoyed if it had been her own publication. When I handed her the book, she moved to a little bench she called her "jury rig." It sat between two file cabinets. The afternoon sun streamed in through a large window behind the bench. Sitting with her back to the window, she could feel the warmth, and sat so the sunlight would come over her shoulder. Virginia positioned the book a foot or more in front of her face. She moved it slowly up, and over, and down, following it with her eyes. I never realized until then that blindness is not necessarily just *black*. She tried for several minutes, to catch a glimpse of color or outline of the book, but she finally declared, "It's no use."

With the resilience I'd seen before, she immediately asked if I would be good enough to read the book to her! Would I? Nothing could have pleased me more. I began that day, and returned each week to read a chapter or two.

It must be true that poets have an instinctive sense of relationships. Virginia demonstrated that to me several times. The first time came when I announced that we had reached the final chapter of the Host book. With her face serious, almost grim, she said, "You haven't mentioned the Host's wife. I recall Chaucer's description of her as a hard, cruel person." She paused for a moment, as if waiting for something to come into focus, then added, "She must be the Church!"

Virginia could feel Chaucer's plan before I disclosed it. It had to be her poet's thought process. The Host's wife, who is easily angered, vicious, and fearful if offended—as an image of the Church—still devastates me. (Reading my Chaucer books to her gave me a rare pleasure. Her quick perception would surprise me in each of them.)

As I prepared to leave that day, she said she'd send me a little unpublished poem she'd written about Chaucer. It arrived in the mail two days later.

```
Chaucer, your poems our endless praises earn.
Phrases, like comets through the centuries burn.
"The lyf so short, the craft so long to lerne."
And every English April, you return.
```

Good luck to the book!

Virgi[nia]

Now, with the book in print, Virginia believed a friend, a professor of English in New York, could be encouraged to "discover" me. For his birthday she sent him a copy of the Host book, expecting he would want to promote this new insight. It didn't happen quite that way. Rather than a new path to opportunity, it turned out to be a dead end. The professor's wife (a woman Virginia knew well) refused to give him the book, because "he doesn't have time to get into that." Virginia, though heartily disappointed, rallied. She gave copies of the book to other friends, hoping to stir up their interest.

Mid-1999 found me in the pre-publication throes of my second book—the one about Chaucer himself and the stories he tells during the pilgrimage. As I read this second book to Virginia, we had reached the story with Sir Elephant (the one rejected by several journals). Her grasp of Chaucer's plan got ahead of me again. I made clear the sexual basis of the story. Then, when I asserted that Sir Elephant *had* to be a physical threat to sexual activity, Virginia exclaimed, "Don't tell me he's Elephantiasis!" and started to laugh.

I pretended to scold, "Virginia, I haven't prepared you to know that yet. It's not fair!" Then, I laughed too. She explained she'd once seen a man afflicted with Elephantiasis—an unforgettable sight.

I usually left her an hour or so before dinnertime at Pilgrim Place. We'd had such a rollicking time that afternoon that she asked if I'd like something to drink before I left. I refused saying that I'd just get going. She pursued the subject a bit more. "I usually have a martini before dinner, and thought you might like to join me."

I'd had a martini only once. It smelled and tasted like hair tonic, but I certainly wouldn't deprive myself of this unique privilege. Doing a quick reversal, I said, "Yes, I'll have one." She went to the tiny refrigerator in the corner of her room and took out gin and vermouth, measured and poured amounts into a glass beaker and stirred the concoction. Taking down two stemmed glasses from the cupboard just above, she set them on the counter, then groped in the refrigerator for the jar of olives which seemed to be in the wrong place. I asked if I could help find it, and handed it to her. She placed a large olive in each glass, and poured in the prepared mixture. It was really terrible, but, at this extraordinary moment, I enjoyed it immensely.

* * *

As we approached the year 2000, which would be Chaucer's 600th anniversary, Virginia and I had some serious conversations about the apparent waning of interest in Chaucer's writing. I took it upon myself to do a survey of Chaucer courses offered locally. I'll give more details in a little while, but, for now, I reported to Virginia that not one course completely dedicated to Chaucer could be found in our area, not even at the colleges of "high reputation." The news appalled her. I knew it would. With instant self-assurance and certainty she announced, "We must organize a Chaucer contest to stimulate interest."

It appeared to be a good idea, but I knew nothing about how to begin. Virginia suggested I get in touch with a couple of organizations or publications concerned with Chaucer. We would offer them the idea, propose the question to be used for the contest, and donate the prize. That all sounded doable, but composing the question brought the two of us to our one and only point of disagreement. I suggested, "Why, after 600 years, is it still important to study Chaucer?" Virginia considered that question trivial. She believed a scholarly comparison, or the analysis of a particular work should be our aim. I could not agree. I saw my question, rather than trivial, as dealing with fundamentals. The answer could be influential, thought-provoking.

She finally relented, and I began a search for the group to run the contest for us. When I discovered the New Chaucer Society, the search ended. Their trustees agreed that such a competition would enhance the upcoming Chaucer 600th anniversary celebration in London, in July of 2000. Virginia and I sent them our agreed-upon question and the prize money. We asked that both faculty and students be allowed to compete. It pleased me that the entry of a graduate student, Robert Meyer-Lee, won the prize.

Matters having to do with Chaucer filled the year 2000 to the brim. I had made up a little guessing game about the zodiac figures I already recognized, and played the game with friends who were quite successful at seeing the answer. When I sent my publisher the zodiac game, he saw the answer and agreed to publish that third book in time for the date of Chaucer's anniversary—October 25, 2000. I read the introduction for that book, which includes the zodiac game, to Virginia. She listened intently. When I asked if she had identified any of the images, the bull was clear to her. Then I asked who the two brothers were, and she said "Gemini." A moment later, she realized that constellations were masquerading as pilgrims. The creativity of the poet's plan captivated her.

The finished book about the zodiac arrived from the publisher by mid-October. I gave a presentation about it to a capacity audience at our city library. Virginia had never attended a library event, mainly because of health issues. You can imagine the surprise and elation of the library manager, Mr. Charles Kaufman, when Virginia, escorted by two friends, arrived to hear me speak.

A few days later, on October 25, we had the ultimate festive event—a Mass in honor of Chaucer followed by a reception. Because Virginia could not attend that evening, I took some of the pasties (made from a medieval recipe) and a bottle of mead to her apartment the next day. She invited the two friends, Judy and Connie, who had escorted her to the library, to join us. The four of us had a grand time toasting Chaucer and munching pasties.

Two weeks later I received the following recollection composed by Virginia in honor of our little celebration.

> *Tribute to Chaucer's Champion*
> *(for Dolores Cullen)*
>
> *For twenty-five years you tried to coax Chaucer from his grave.*
> *On the road to Canterbury, he smiled benignly at your efforts.*
> *Nobody in his day had heard of California but you succeeded in the resurrection of a noble name.*
> *And as six hundred years gathered bits and pieces of his poems, you gave them a new twist.*
> *Why was his smile so full of mischief?*
> *Only you guessed the riddles; you had the key.*
> *And we paid tribute with Chaucer's favorite beverage: mead, delicate as honeysuckle.*
> *And you brought mushroom pasties you had made, full of medieval grace.*
> *We filled tiny tumblers in salute to a great poet and a worthy interpreter.*
>
> —Nov. 8, 2000 Virginia Hamilton Adair

What a special keepsake!

Over the years of our friendship, Virginia expressed her disappointment a number of times, saying "Elliott should have…" She alluded to my Chaucer professor's failure to provide me with an introduction to the academic world. I could only say, "It doesn't matter what *should have* happened. It didn't."

In January of 2001, all I had wanted to say about the Canterbury Pilgrims had made it into print. Virginia, a few weeks shy of her eighty-eighth birthday, wrote a letter recommending me to Dr. Bob Suzuki, the President of Cal Poly. I received a copy of the letter from her. It said, "I would like to bring to your attention the work of a former student of mine, Dolores Cullen." She noted the titles of my books and said, "This is a student alumna that should make the Cal Poly English Department rejoice," and, "It is time Cal Poly took notice of this remarkable woman." Below her signature it said, "Virginia Hamilton Adair, Professor Emeritus, Cal Poly English Department."

This, her final effort on my behalf, did have a positive effect at Cal Poly. After her letter, the college library took notice of my publications in their annual recognition ceremony. In addition, I participated in the Alumni Association's yearly "Professor for a Day" program. It gives me the annual privilege of talking to Cal Poly students about my insight.

I continued to see Virginia every month or so to tell her of the latest happenings. Her family had a special ninetieth birthday celebration for her. Because she felt uneasy in a crowd, and we all understood that, she sat in a comfortable chair in a corner of the large room. We took turns sitting next to her, one or two at a time, to individually extend our good wishes. I told her afterward that she looked like a mother-confessor—and we, a succession of penitents. The picture amused her.

She died in 2004, her ninety-first year. Her daughter sent me a note that said Virginia "enjoyed working on Chaucer with you." She had made all the difference in my life. Not until then did I recognize that I had made a difference for Virginia.

VI.

Search for a Publisher

Now that we've established Virginia's essential presence as the cheering section for my Chaucer adventure, we'll take a time-leap back to 1994, to the moment she and I became friends on a first-name basis. I saw her regularly after that to keep her posted about the story I'll tell you now.

Dealing with the subject of the Host, which I'd thought about and worked on for twenty-five years, I had a fair idea where the holes were that needed to be filled in with facts for the book I planned to write. The answer to the *how* of what Chaucer did is *allegory*. The *why* is something else. I would search Scripture, the *Middle English Dictionary*, plays from the Middle Ages, and medieval legends and prayers, as well, for ideas that inspired Chaucer.

This Host *not being recognized* as Christ, is a pattern found in the Bible. Mary Magdalene took the risen Christ to be a gardener (John 20:14–15). And, even more to the situation Chaucer creates, the apostles, who met Christ traveling to Emmaus, thought him just a pilgrim, a stranger (Luke 24:15–18). A second idea from Scripture explains why the Host is "the most *enveloped* in sin." As Christ, he has taken all the sins of the world *upon* himself.

Then there are important definitions in the *Middle English Dictionary*. One alludes to the tradition of the Mystical Body. In this context the Host offering the pilgrims his "head" can be seen as Christ indicating his function as *head* of the body "mystik." And, although the Host's claim "the substance is in me" is generally considered unclear today, clarity is found in the MED definition of *substance*. The word, in relation to theology, refers to "the Incarnate Christ."

From medieval dramas, I learned the importance of the Host's exclaiming "Harrow! by nails and by blood!" Though footnotes in modern texts may find the expression "obscure," the medieval explanation is obvious. In the play called "The Harrowing of Hell," the action follows Christ (after being crucified *by nails and by blood*) down to the gates of hell where he smashes them (he harrows hell). Thus, he releases the souls who have been waiting for the Redeemer. The Host's reference is both startling and powerful when the words are understood to be said by Christ.

It also surprised me to see how clearly the pattern of participants in a medieval *Corpus Christi* procession echoed the image of Chaucer's pilgrim journeyers. Dramatized *Corpus Christi* stories, intermittently performed as the procession moves, are similar to the Canterbury pilgrims' narrations presented as they travel.

In *Panis Angelicus*, a popular hymn written centuries ago by Thomas Aquinas for the Feast of Corpus Christi, I found that Christ is asked to be the guide of pilgrims to their journey's end. That is surely represented in the Canterbury plan.

Collections of stories (*Gesta Romanorum* and *The Golden Legend)* include legends of Christ's wife (the Church), so for the Host to have a wife comes as no surprise. It confirms that mode of thinking before the year 1400. To make claims about the Host believable as reflections of Christ, the time element is essential.

Religious poems, in a very simple fashion, speak of Christ as a "householder" who feeds and shelters "his folk." That's the initial picture Chaucer gives us. But the poem that really binds all the strands of Christ's description to Chaucer's Host is Number 36 in a fourteenth-century anthology by Carleton Brown. The lines speak of Christ with his wife, a victorious hero (harrowing hell), a powerful business man (as is the Host with his lodging), who has bought mankind (by shedding his blood). The final image is Christ as a blessed pilgrim. Could details of Chaucer's Host be more completely Christ?

Now for *why* Chaucer would have written this allegory. Writers often resorted to allegory in times of repressive control. The two levels of meaning were designed to outwit harsh authority.

England's Merciless Parliament or threats of the Inquisition constituted such repression. But why would Chaucer choose to conceal a message when discovery could result in death, perhaps even by fearful means? The answer is that it was a matter of conscience.

A responsible Christian, who had important information, *must* impart it to others. The Middle Ages taught a moral responsibility to share what is received from God, not only material goods but insight, knowledge. When I read of the great medieval philosopher Alan de Lille's warning that possession of knowledge makes it a duty to share it—one commits a sin of omission "who shutteth knowledge in his mouth"—that explained Chaucer's choosing to live his days in a sense of jeopardy. There is no doubt the poet gained special knowledge from his travels and his closeness to the crown. We are not talking of comic criticism—of poking fun at hypothetical churchmen—but of covert denunciation aimed at the very core of the Church itself. Accusations against the authority of the Church held great personal risk, but a certainty of eternal reparation would be far worse. God, in the hereafter, would hold him accountable.

I believe Chaucer took his salvation seriously. That's the message I find illustrated in his narration of a profligate life (in *Thopas*), which was halted by the Host, that is, by Christ. The interruption is followed by a resolve of repentance (in *Melibee*). I am certain Chaucer knew he might forfeit his life if those in power understood the concealed intention. It is his courage and genius that are the basis of my passion to make his message known.

As the Host book neared completion, I felt it needed to be read by someone well-acquainted with medieval literature. Professor Dick Barnes, who had delivered *Cursor Mundi* to my door, came to mind. I visited his office to ask if he'd be willing, and he agreed. When I inquired as to the cost, he smiled and said, "You couldn't afford me, but I'll be glad to do it as a favor." Though, in the end, not as enthusiastic as Virginia about the content, he did call it "a good read."

I had packed proof upon proof into one-hundred-eighty pages

of text, and another seventy-five pages of notes and bibliography. With the manuscript read by Professor Barnes, the pages checked and checked again by the San Dimas writers, it was October 1995 and time for the book to face the world.

Poring over *The Writer's Market* for several hours, I created a list of publishers who dealt with the category of literary criticism. That's what I was doing, analyzing, criticizing a piece of literature!

I began with contacting academic presses because, I reasoned, my ideas were appropriate for higher education. Often I'd get a quick rejection, within a month, denoting either efficiency or indifference. Then, one day, I realized, without "Ph.D." after my name, and with all the pressure on academics to publish, professors and would-be professors with a university return address were probably given preference by editors when apportioning time for reading manuscripts.

With that realization, I put aside the list of academic publishers in spring of 1996 and concentrated on the list of small presses who dealt with literary criticism. On my way to the writers' group, I'd stop at the post office every couple of weeks to send off another hopeful packet. Each publisher has preferences, like a query and synopsis, or a synopsis and one chapter, or some other combination. I'd follow the requirements and always include a return envelope. From the beginning of this mailing process, however, I thought it better for my morale not to count the number of rejections as they regularly came to my mailbox. The enclosed letters were quite consistent. As slight variations on a theme, they said, "Thank you for thinking of us; your manuscript does not fit our current needs; but good luck." I'd keep Virginia posted about my ongoing efforts.

And, because the pressure of time—the fragile nature of life—is always with me, when I began to send out book one, I started to write the second book, the book about the poet himself. That's the next step of the plan spelled out back in 1972 during the "dream," where I rode in a coach with Virginia.

* * *

When I say I didn't count the times the manuscript returned, I don't mean to imply that the rejections had no effect on me. Counting them, however, made no sense. I couldn't allow numbers to stop me. I had a special job to do, and I'd give it my best shot. This cartoon, from our local newspaper, felt like it was intended just for me. I tacked it up in clear view. It still makes me chuckle.

DON'T EVER GIVE UP!!!

The new book, about the poet himself, had a decidedly different personality from the Host book. The first had a somewhat heavenly ambiance, while the second got downright earthy. It begins with Chaucer as the "narrator" of the *General Prologue*, the introduction to the *Tales*. Every time the words tripped me up, I'd stop, look at the surrounding words, and try to figure what sort of trick it might be. In less than two pages, I discovered that the action does not take place in real time—nor at a specific location!

No matter how real the considerable amount of apparent "action" appears, it is a fantasy.

Chaucer had worked with fantasy before. He did a great practice piece called *The House of Fame*. Much of that story finds Chaucer on a tour of the universe while aloft astride the back of an eagle! That and the *General Prologue* are about as sci-fi as today's fiction. The poet's genius is boundless. It's greater than the credit given him by most readers (and many scholars).

In this pilgrimage outside time or place, Chaucer presents a splendid panorama of the overnight guests doing many things, in many places, but none in the here and now. We learn much about the events of their lives and quirks of their personalities. Their arrival at the lodging, or a description of their luggage or accommodations are deemed irrelevant. Even a Pilgrim's features and clothing—except for a few details that serve Chaucer's purpose—play a small part. I learned a great deal about these random but purposeful details. They are the main feature of book three.

Another oddity of Chaucer's plan is making himself part of a motley group, the only such group among the journeyers. They are the last five Pilgrims to be introduced and have the most unsavory personalities of all the travelers. Each is repulsive. They steal, lie, swindle, fornicate, and prey upon the poor. There has to be a reason for his associating himself with this handful of scoundrels.

Interestingly, dealing with Chaucer in the real world, the brief biography in my old college text made a passing reference to legal action taken against the poet by a woman, Cecilia Chaumpaigne. The 1968 Britannica, on my shelf, says not a word about her. Odd. The scholar who updated the Chaucer entry for the 1974 Britannica (at the library) inserted two sentences about the lady, flavored by the suggestion that we refrain from seeing the poet guilty as charged. That had to be a lead to investigate.

I discovered that a lawyer named Watts, in the 1940s, studied and wrote about the case of Cecilia. The poet is charged with *raptus*, a word that needs interpretation. Watts is sure the word intends "rape." He also found that Chaucer scholars soft-pedal that idea, or deny it completely with no grounds whatever for denial.

At the conclusion of his investigation, a question remained for Watts. Why, he wondered (according to the structure of the medieval court system), did the king seem to ignore the matter of a felony charged against Chaucer? More recent sleuthing of Professor Christopher Cannon, in the 1990s, revealed the answer to Watts' question.

The answer unearthed by Cannon, has to do with documents. The original charge of *raptus* appeared in Chancery. Three days later, recorded at King's Bench (documents the king would be most likely to see), the words were manipulated—and *raptus* omitted. One can only speculate as to how that came about. It seems likely that Chaucer's friends at court may have used their influence to protect him. And Cannon agreed with Watts that all the evidence points to *raptus* as rape.

Creative and imaginative scholars have gone so far as to cast Chaucer as some sort of hero where Cecilia is concerned. Wishful thinking aside, the poet can be seen as a man who took advantage of a woman, and that is that. Is this felonious recollection what caused him to place himself in the midst of five scoundrels? It seems likely. Though he doesn't report a personal flaw in the *General Prologue* introduction, Pilgrim Chaucer will soon elaborate, for the reader's benefit, on a less-than-wholesome past.

Bringing to mind the classic structure that says a story must have a beginning, a middle, and an end, Chaucer makes a personal appearance at each of those positions. He arrives at the Tabard first, says the concluding prayer, and at the mid-point of the journey it is *his* story we hear. That story is the pricking endeavors of Thopas, the activities I explicated but journals declined to publish.

Doing a proper job with Chaucer's own story demanded a diligent effort. A dedicated researcher must, at times, be courageous. I would have to endure the hardship of reading hundreds of old bawdy ballads and obscene riddles, to prepare myself with adequate background to face the medieval sexual wordplay that lay ahead of me. Posterity can thank the poet Robert Burns and other diligent collectors of ribald ballads for the wealth of earthy, erotic lyrics preserved for us. My reading list also required acquainting myself with Old English obscene riddles. And, for good measure, I'd delve into Chauliac's medical description of medieval beliefs about sexuality, conception, and venereal disease.

Burns, in the 1700s, had done Scotland and the world a service by transcribing the words of robust Scottish peasant songs he loved. One warned young men not to spend too much time in the saddle—no matter how soft they found it. Another tells of a well-known ploughman who had three oxen—one long, and the other two plump and round.

A collection of ballads from the 1500s told of a ferret that seeks out holes in which to hide, and of the admired Tom Longe who delivers merchandise. The MED played its part by providing a direct answer to a precise problem when it told of a rascal who stands erect, no longer wearing his hood. Feminine depictions might be a box, a well, a mouse trap, a room to let, and other fanciful receptacles.

In rereading the story about Thopas' time *spent in the saddle*, I came to a sudden understanding of Chaucer's scheme. My journal relates.

> I sat down to reread the Tale of Thopas. About one page into the story, I read these lines:
>
> > His fair steede in his prykynge
> > *So swatte* that men might him wrynge;*
> > His sides were al blood.
>
> The visual image in my mind is *not* a horse. With all the terminology and description that has gone before, we are being told the adventures of male genitalia! I'd never seen it so clearly before.

When I presented the chapter about Thopas to the San Dimas

---

*sweat, or exert oneself

writers, I prefaced it by saying, "If I didn't know you all so well, I'd be too embarrassed to read this." (My publisher later said it was the most explicit book he'd ever published!) Broad images like Chaucer's were, no doubt, familiarly passed down verbally from generation to generation.

When the San Dimas writers accepted the Thopas chapter, I sent it to my youngest daughter for her opinion. How would the grandchildren receive it? She said, "Mom, the kids know all about that stuff."

"Yes, I know that," I assured her. "What I'm concerned about is—do they realize their *grandmother* knows?" She laughed and cheered me on. With her endorsement of the spicy content, I continued.

Seeing Thopas as Chaucer's admission of sexual misconduct, when the Host—Christ—interrupts the narration, this action of Christ constitutes a scene of conversion. Chaucer's offering which follows bears this out. His second story is heavy with morality, theology, and philosophy. The story he adapted was a popular prose treatise in medieval French, which he translated into English, modifying it to change its emphasis. It fascinated me to compare the French text (in *Sources and Analogues*) to Chaucer's words. With subtle alterations, the poet makes the story his own. The Host—Christ—accepts Chaucer's second story which illustrates the poet has changed his thinking and behavior. This pair of stories are two sides of a coin. The double offering is one unit.

While I worked on the second book, I continued to send out the Host book, over and over. After more than a year of mailings, I had only one publisher left on my list, a small press in Santa Barbara. I sent them the Host book in May of 1997. I knew I would soon have to revisit *The Writer's Market* to find additional publishers, but I would wait on making up a new list because I had formulated a plan for a once-in-a-lifetime trip. If I attended the Franciscan convention to be held on the east coast in July, and returned by way of Chicago in August, my family and I could celebrate on my fiftieth wedding anniversary at the church where I had been married.

I had just begun to organize the many particulars for the trip when the long-awaited moment arrived. The date? Unforgettable Tuesday, June 17, 1997. The mailman delivered a reply from John Daniel, the Santa Barbara publisher. He hadn't sent a variation on that standard theme; he had, instead, composed music to delight my ears and my spirit. "I wish my brother had lived to read your book," he wrote. His brother had been a medievalist and chairman of a university English department. John Daniel had understood, and wanted to see the entire manuscript! It has been a long time since that letter arrived, but I still tingle to remember his words.

The next day became a whirlwind of activity. I mailed the manuscript to Mr. Daniel. And I made hotel and travel reservations for my trip. And, to be practical, I scheduled a medical check up. Didn't want to get to Boston and find my medication needed adjustment, or some such.

My doctor ordered a couple of x-rays and the usual lab tests, just routine. But a week later, she asked to see me. They had "found something" were her words. There went the fiftieth anniversary celebration and the rest of the trip. We planned surgery instead. Do you recall the twenty-fifth anniversary where the celebratory lasagna ended up in the freezer? In case you're wondering, I have already made up my mind NOT to make any plans for my seventy-fifth anniversary. I don't want to be disappointed a third time.

Before reporting to the hospital, I had book requirements to be seen to. My San Dimas writer friends did extra duty to help get book two, about Chaucer the pilgrim, in good order.

Another matter dealt with the first book (the Host book). I wanted to compose the dedication page and send it to John Daniel; I had enclosed a note with the manuscript to tell him to expect a note about the dedicatee. You may remember my visit with Virginia to ask if I could name her. She listened, and after her peppery response to "mind your humility," acquiesced. This is where that scene fits in. When I got home after talking with her, I set down the following words on a sheet of paper and enclosed a short identifying note for John Daniel:

> *For*
> *Ted, my husband*
> *and*
> *Virginia Hamilton Adair*
> *because they were there for me*
> *from the beginning*

That completed the final touch for the Host book. When I mailed the dedication, everything on my to-do list had been checked off. Now I could turn my attention to the medical event before me.

After surgery, there were complications. The estimated five-day stay, quoted to me, actually became three weeks. When I belatedly arrived home, I found a letter from Santa Barbara, in the stack of mail waiting for me. It was an offer of a contract to publish the Host book. To make up for lost time, as soon as I'd read the letter, I *phoned* John Daniel to accept. He'd be happy to send the contract right out. I didn't mention my medical problem to him. Why complicate things?

It's a good thing we can't see the future, because twenty-four hours later I had the ER on my agenda. This time I acquired a pacemaker and another assortment of complications. Another surgery would set everything right, they told me. During the night before going into that surgery, I had a very special surprise: one of my daughters retrieved the book contract, which by that time had been delivered to my house, and brought it to me at the hospital. She figured my mind would be more at ease if I had signed the contract before the operation. She mailed it to John Daniel at Fithian Press on her way home that night.

The whole family had a tough summer. Driving in California generally means long distances—and we were in the midst of a heat wave. The hospital sojourn seemed endless. I finally told my handsome, be-turbaned cardiologist (who had studied Chaucer in India!) that I *had* to get home. "I've just signed my first book contract," I announced, hoping to influence him. Though sympathetic and happy for me, he didn't budge.

Liberation finally came at the end of September. I'd been away so long that my kitchen seemed foreign to me. Anticipation of seeing *Chaucer's Host: Up-So-Doun* in print, as you can imagine, went a long way to aid my recovery, but I had no time to dawdle. The evening of my return home, I called Judy Wenrick, whose Mac demonstration had put me on the right computer track. She and I had studied for our Master's Degrees together at Cal Poly. I asked if she would scrutinize the manuscript for my second book. "I'd love to. I'm so glad to hear you're at home." Knowing the urgency I felt, she readily agreed, "I'll stop by right after I finish teaching tomorrow."

The publishing process for book one had begun, but book two had a long way to go to be ready for consideration by a publisher. Judy and I chatted briefly about this second book which I called "Pilgrim Chaucer: Center Stage." I chose the title because the poet is really the one and only entertainer in the *Canterbury Tales*. From beginning to end, he holds the spotlight whether he is narrating, or relaying what he saw, or what he heard from the Pilgrims. The title pleased Judy. She stayed only a short time, partly because she had so many things to do, but also out of concern for my low energy reserve. I'll admit I certainly didn't look my best. I was just glad to be home.

The first week of October, John Daniel requested "a diskette of the manuscript [for the Host book] in *rich text format*." I understood about back-up disks for your writing, but "rich text" meant nothing. My son, with a few special clicks, produced the requested disk, slipped it into a mailer, and took care of sending it, "certified," of course. At this point, with dreams coming true, you don't take chances with your brainchildren.

A special problem had to be dealt with because of the Middle English in the Host book. Two letters that are part of the Middle English alphabet—*thorn* and *yogh*—have dropped from use. *Thorn* became *th; yogh*, developed into *y* or *g*. These obsolete characters were present in many of my Chaucer quotes. In preparing the manuscript, I got around that by substituting a subscripted *3* which looked similar to the *yogh,* and by using the overstrike feature to create a *p* which had a "stick" projecting above the line, as well as below the line. It made an adequate *thorn*. That worked well for me, but it didn't translate properly for publishing. The letters were not available in any font, at that time, so Eric, the book designer, had to have the *thorn* and *yogh* created. (I sent him a photocopied page with examples, as a guide.)

By mid-October, my recuperation was going well. So, the evening Judy brought back the "Pilgrim Chaucer" manuscript we talked for quite a while, as we munched the cookies I had made that morning. The book needed work, especially the analogy I had used to show how closely the stories of Thopas and Melibee are associated. I described them as Siamese twins (the old term which later became *conjoined twins*). Judy, always ready to give a truthful opinion, shook her head and objected, "I'm sorry, but that image offends me."

That needed some thought. The story certainly had to have *something* to maintain a reader's interest as you leave racy Thopas and turn to plodding, philosophical Melibee. It's very much like a day in the country as you skip along in the sunshine, but suddenly the sky turns dark and you find yourself slogging knee-deep through a marsh. How can you continue to enjoy your outing?

A completely unorthodox idea popped into my head. I'd rewrite Melibee as a medieval puppet show. To demonstrate the closeness of the Thopas/Melibee plots, they became a Saturday movie matinee with the Host's interruption creating a cliff-hanger situation that found resolution in Melibee. It took several weeks of work, and substantial reworking, with the advice of the San Dimas writers, to have it shape up. Judy approved this new version.

As I reworked the puppet show, the first proof pages for the Host book were delivered. The quotes from Chaucer, as well as the general text were all set flush with the left margin. The book designer, Eric (Larson), wanted my comments. To see my words in print thrilled me, of course, but I enclosed a note to say, "I assume you don't intend to have all the poetry against the left margin." I returned the pages with my thoughts, and an illustration of centered quotes, the way they *ought* to be.

Eric sent a lengthy reply indicating that "flush left" is the logical and the most attractive way to display poetry. Doing otherwise "makes the whole page look raggedy and disheveled." In addition, the identifying citations following the segment of a poem, when shifted to the right, appear to be "floating in space."

I begged to differ, at length and in detail. My aim is aesthetics, I declared, not logic. And citations identifying the source, when a modest distance from the lines of the poem, are not "floating in space," but are easily distinguished as the sought-after reference. I don't think I've ever been as forceful, before or since. I sent two plans I thought acceptable for page arrangements—neither flush left—and waited. (I had plenty to keep me busy with the Pilgrim Chaucer rewrite.) With Thanksgiving just around the corner the matter would not be resolved quickly. Time off for the holiday brought a natural delay in the publishing progress.

In mid-December, a bulging envelope arrived from Santa Barbara. A printout of pages 180 and 181 of the Host book illustrated the newly created *thorn* and *yogh*. They were just right. The envelope also contained a copy of Professor Dick Barnes' blurb for the back of the book—and the anticipated letter from Eric. He opted for the second plan I had suggested. His letter closed with, "Thanks for your help."

Several months earlier, in September, when a regular exchange of letters between the publisher (Fithian Press) and myself began, we addressed each other as Mr. Daniel, Mr. Larson, and Mrs. Cullen. Now, at year's end 1997, we were John and Eric and Dolores. I couldn't have wanted a relationship of more generosity and integrity.

With January 1998 came a request for author photos. A style-conscious friend insisted I must wear a plain dark top, with, perhaps, a string of pearls. I went along with the advice, sans pearls. A meaningful accent, to complement the black sweater, is the *Middle English Dictionary*, my favorite research tool. My holding it characterized me more than did pearls.

The Host book—if no setback occurred—would be out in July. Many processes were yet to be completed. They were exciting but also laden with responsibility. You have to face the fact that if you miss something as you proof the pages, the oversight becomes permanent printed history!

In February, Susan—Mrs. John Daniel—mailed galley proofs to blurbers, the people who would read this printout and give a response to be part of the back cover. We already had Professor Barnes' "good read" opinion. My cousin suggested Dr. McCray, a college president in her town, who was noted for his interest in Chaucer. He responded with "it meets a need thus far unfulfilled." My son's friend, Hugh Hewitt of PBS TV, asked to read *Chaucer's Host*. He generously proposed that "Cullen's expertise and passion draws in even readers who swore off Chaucer decades ago." One potential blurber never responded, but the three out of four made for a fine assortment of comments.

The second proof pages came to me in late February. Corrections indicated in the first proofing had been made. This readthrough amounted to final approval. I carefully read every word, the Middle English, in particular. Medieval words had to be checked almost letter by letter because of the unpredictable spelling. At this stage, *corrections* could be made, but no *revisions*, no moving text, no changes of any kind were allowed. Content and pagination were set. Even small changes could have a domino effect where succeeding pages, perhaps many of them, would need to be modified. That could throw off the publishing schedule. In a word, alterations were *verboten*. When I mailed the proofs back, that ended my part of the job. Now, Susan took over with publicity and distribution.

The Fithian Press "Catalog of Forthcoming Books" called *Chaucer's Host*, "An intriguing and compelling new interpretation of the central figure in Chaucer's *Canterbury Tales.*" The press release announced "something new in Chaucer studies." Deanna, one of the San Dimas writers, printed out an online description from the Fithian website that says, "Cullen posits a secret identity of Herry Bailly, the keeper of the Tabard…and poses convincingly that Chaucer's Host is none other than Jesus Christ, himself." I learned that *Chaucer's Host* could be purchased through Amazon,

Barnes & Noble, and Borders online. It all came together in such a rush, after marking time for so long.

A small, heavy box arrived from Santa Barbara in the first week of July 1998. I knew what it contained. Alone in my kitchen, I set the box on the table, slit the tape, and folded down the edges of the box. I lifted out a copy of my beautifully finished book. I had pictured being overjoyed, laughing, and dancing around the room with a sense of accomplishment. My spontaneous reaction, however, caught me by surprise. Instead of dancing, I groped for a chair, sat down, hugging *Chaucer's Host* to my breast, and sobbed. I felt the release of almost thirty years of waiting.

Thinking once again of Virginia, if there had never been an English professor who believed in my ideas, who encouraged me to pursue them, I would never have reached that moment of fulfillment. If the "intellectual bottleneck" condition that I lived with at the beginning had never been overcome, if I had continued to work at *containing* the excitement building up inside of me, I don't want to even speculate what the outcome might have been. But that long-awaited moment, thank God, *had* come. For several months, afterward, I basked in the joy of having entered the world of published authors.

Announcements of publication were sent to a long list of relatives, and friends. Susan Daniel sent examination copies of *Chaucer's Host* to local newspapers, book reviewers, and to journals dealing with the medieval world. She dispatched notices of a new slant on Chaucer's work to bookstores at universities with medieval studies departments across the United States and Canada. Professors who teach medieval literature were informed of this lively new reading and were offered complimentary copies of the book. She contacted popular journals with an appeal for Catholic intellectuals as the perfect showcases for presenting *Chaucer's Host* as the embodiment of the Eucharistic Host, guide of pilgrims. Among the variety in her considered roster of publications that might beget reviews were *Modern Maturity, The Creative Woman, The Hungry Mind Review, The Chaucer Review,* and even *The NY Times.* Each received an examination copy of my book.

I enjoyed a flurry of congratulatory notes. My dear friend Rose, who wrote for the *Chicago Sun-Times*, congratulated me and expressed surprise.

> I don't understand the trouble you've had in getting your ideas about Chaucer accepted—except that academics often get lost in details and don't see, or even look at, the main themes of the works they deal with. From the perspective of an ordinary reader, your thoughts have never seemed far-fetched at all, but rather reasonable and even self-evident. (Maybe you have to be a believer.)

Ron, who taught on the East Coast, had kind words.

> You do a fine job of approaching a genuinely lay (nonacademic) audience—explaining things clearly and interestingly so that a reader can pick up your enthusiasm and curiosity.... The backgrounding was extensive and not at all easy to accomplish for a contemporary audience...but you come through it with a confident good humor that keeps the reader with you. The voice is wonderful—personal, engaging, patient, and so very much a Chaucer fan. It projects the image of an interesting, intelligent, inquiring person of considerable charm. No wonder, I say.

Visits with both Rose and Ron would have been included on that trip that never was.

The October 1998 issue of *The Midwest Review* said, "Written to be immediately accessible to the non-specialist general reader, Cullen's new insight will compel significant reassessment within the scholarly community of Chaucer studies." The accompanying letter told of their review being posted on internet bookstores and forwarded to Gale Research. (Gale, eventually, included my biography in their reference work *Contemporary Authors*.)

Rather as a lark, I went to our city library to ask about *Chaucer's Host*, just for the fun of seeing it on the shelf. I asked the reference librarian about author Dolores Cullen, and a book called *Chaucer's Host*. After studying her computer screen, she wrote on a small slip of paper PR 1875 H67 C85 1998 and the title *Chaucer's Ghost!* I was too amused to correct her. And, for good measure, I got a notice from Fithian Press that there is "a special page for your book on our website." Unfortunately, I couldn't see it. No internet connection yet. My days were too full to take on a new project.

As a final touch to the story of *Chaucer's Host*, I had two celebratory T-shirts made. Printed on the back of each were the words, "Chaucer spoken here." I kept one, and sent the other to Dr. Mike Nelson, M.D. He had talked Chaucer to me, while I lay on a gurney in the ER the year before. I wanted him to know I had completely recovered and had written my book. It was a different, but sincere "thank you."

Enough of drinking in the heady brew of success. The time had come to return my full attention to the still-in-progress "Pilgrim Chaucer." Even while celebrating part-time, I had maintained a schedule of polishing up this second volume with my writer friends each week. With the second book near completion by mid-October, I called John Daniel to ask if he'd be interested in looking at another project of mine. Certainly. I sent all of "Pilgrim Chaucer" on October 20.

To my surprise, John's reply arrived a mere ten days later. Once again he had read and understood the significance of my Chaucer thinking. He called it "revolutionary, door-opening theories" and in regard to this second manuscript, he closed with "whenever you are ready, it will be my pleasure."

On November 5, 1998 I signed the contract for *Pilgrim Chaucer*. Posted in large letters at the back of my mind was the date October 2000—Chaucer's 600th anniversary. Thinking about the third (the final) volume, I couldn't resist asking, just for my own information really, "If a book were to be published in October 2000, when should it be in your hands for consideration?" John calculated that he'd want it one year before. The size of the project rather overwhelmed me, but I had to give it some thought. Could

I actually get the third book of the dream written in time? What a target to aim for!

If I made telling the story of all the Pilgrims my goal, the months from November 1998 until October 1999 would call for double-duty. I had worked on, and finished writing book two, *Pilgrim Chaucer*, while being involved with proofreading and composing little items, such as the dedication and acknowledgments, for *Chaucer's Host*. With the experience of that first run-through, I knew, more or less, the tasks expected of me as *Pilgrim Chaucer* went into production. This third volume, about the rest of the travelers, however, held a greater challenge than the first two had. While *Chaucer's Host* and *Pilgrim Chaucer* were each about a single main character, the third volume dealt with demonstrating the alternate identities for not one, not two, but *twenty-nine pilgrims*.

Before making the decision to try, I needed to know if other people were able to "see" the double images I saw in Chaucer's words. To get an idea of whether that quirk in my imagination—that responded to Chaucer's hidden images—was shared by others, I constructed a little game and tried it with small groups, including the San Dimas writers. *It worked.* The pictures Chaucer's words created in my mind, my friends could see in their minds, too. How exciting! The game players were intrigued. They wanted to know more, and wanted to know *why* the images are double. That made up my mind. I had to dedicate the coming year to telling the story of this new way of seeing Chaucer's Pilgrims.

Length would be only one reason to wonder if it could all be brought together by the October 1999 deadline. Another and greater challenge was the fact that the major portion of the research *had not yet been done.*

Figuring the publishing process for the second book (*Pilgrim Chaucer*), which had just begun, would be similar to that of the first, I determined that anything regarding book two would get my complete and speedy attention as soon as it came up. That way I wouldn't be distracted by a responsibility hanging over my head. As I completed each set of proof pages, or anything else assigned, I'd resume the pursuit of facts new and fascinating about the Pilgrims and all sorts of information that naturally branched out from what I found. I read about mythology, and how people of the Middle Ages adapted traditional visual images of pagan gods for Christian purposes (handsome Apollo might be used to represent the figure of Christ); and about astrology, which combined with astronomy and encouraged seeing planets as both gods *and* planets *simultaneously*. I needed to see time as cyclic, rather than my usual thought of time as a straight line of day by day progression. Reference works I used documented classic authors and works that Chaucer had read; I could trust the authority of such writings.

In the spring of 1999, I wrote to Annie Dillard, the renowned author and a great inspiration to me, asking if she'd write a blurb for the second book. She declined, but wished me luck. Two excellent blurbers, however, did come through. Jan Bartholome, Editor in Chief of a local newspaper said, "Dolores Cullen has achieved the impossible with *Pilgrim Chaucer: Center Stage*: she has sparked within me a real fascination for the works of Geoffrey Chaucer. What my literature professor made incredibly boring is brought to life…" And, dear friend Judy Wenrick, a consultant for the Writing Project at the University of California at Riverside, said that *Pilgrim Chaucer* would inspire "writing students to view scholarship as an adventurous and creative endeavor. Cullen's prose radiates with the reflective voice of a writer unafraid to chart her own course."

An unexpected bonus for *Pilgrim Chaucer* came to light just before the second proof pages were printed. In my search for new pilgrim information at the Claremont School of Theology, I found a copy of the *Wyclif Bible,* which dates from the Middle Ages and is written in English. (Several libraries, including Honnold and the Claremont School of Theology, are part of a system known as "The Libraries of the Claremont Colleges.") While perusing this Bible, I found an unexpected tidbit I couldn't ignore. Eric added that tidbit to an adaptable footnote without a problem. The *Wyclif Bible* warns of "daughters who open their quivers to every arrow." The image fits the Thopas hunter theme like an archer's glove.

Though there were continuing complications involving book three and the pilgrim quest, I had no concerns regarding *Pilgrim Chaucer*. Eric settled the question of the cover design when he found a polite, slightly suggestive, little grotesque to greet the reading public. And he recommended *hunter* green for the color, our "in" joke. Chaucer's name is related to the French word *chausseur*, which means *hunter*. The volume is dedicated, in gratitude, to Professor Dick Barnes.

I'm thankful that no serious problem arose with book two to distract me from my concentration on book three. As soon as my responsibilities with *Pilgrim Chaucer* were over, I moved into a 10-to-10 mode. Family and friends adjusted quickly. It meant they could reach me by phone before ten in the morning, or after ten in the evening, but not in between. Not that I worked all the time, sometimes I napped and didn't want to be disturbed. Consider that in a few months, through the capability and generosity of two of my granddaughters, I would be endowed with my first two great-grandchildren! Naps were a daily elixir for this grey-haired night owl.

As I approached the cast of Pilgrims, the precise identity of a few zodiac figures and planets was certain, but I had not yet recognized *all* of them. Filling in the complete pattern would take time, time needed to sift through and ponder each of Chaucer's clues. Who is the Clerk (scholar), for example, or who is the Yeoman who serves the fleeting Canon (clergyman)? As a matter of fact, what part does the other Yeoman play who serves the Knight? Without doubt the Knight portrays Mars, but what hidden purpose could his Yeoman, his servant, have? Such queries go on indefinitely. Answers to those questions, and many, many more, had to be found. I could foresee hours and hours spent at the Honnold Library, hours interwoven with proofreading *Pilgrim Chaucer*. Honnold had been, and continued to be, the source for more than ninety percent of the information that filled my pages. Its staff guided me through an ever-lengthening list of subjects I worked with, or discovered. I found the core of each Pilgrim to be unique; each constituted a new quest; the diverse pursuit became my education. Ideas piled up and then, suddenly shifted, as my journal relates, *"of their own volition"* to display a significance and a pattern I hadn't seen before. *"It was rather like a kaleidoscope—I passively, but attentively, gazed in amazement as the particles moved into glorious revelations."* Born with an instinct to satisfy my intellectual curiosities, my memory of that year is an unforgettable thrill.

At times my quest about the pilgrims led me far afield to rare books beyond Honnold's sizable holdings. Being neither a faculty member nor an enrolled student, I had no interlibrary loan privileges. If an unusual source appeared promising, how could I obtain the promise it held? Fortunately, several graduate students and Honnold librarians—all of whom shall remain nameless—were enthusiastic about my ideas. The exceptional volumes on my *must see* list were requested by them in their own names. I'd use the borrowed book in the library, or an accommodating friend would bring it to my home and retrieve it a few days later.

I considered myself fortunate to have friends with skills I needed, but lacked myself. Latin translations were provided by Victor or Ted. Sabrina spoke French fluently. And for seeing a comet under the best circumstances, I relied on John's advice; he taught astronomy.

Except for the "game," I'd done no writing and very little thinking about what had to be accomplished to prepare the third manuscript. The collected information grew steadily. Remember those cigar boxes each labeled with the name of a Pilgrim? The boxes became the center of activity. It seemed no matter what I read, the subject would touch upon other fascinating fields, many parallel subjects which reflected Chaucer's legendary encyclopedic knowledge. (He might be called a "Renaissance Man," but the Renaissance had not yet happened.) I'd jot down facts, or page numbers for making photocopies, or add names of books to my *must see* list, and slip each jotting into the properly labeled box. Reading and organizing all the notes took a while before the writing could begin. The wealth of material became richer and richer before the time came to invest the assets I'd accumulated.

On the practical side, I also had to discover a "hook" to grab a reader's interest. The game turned out to be the natural lead in. (In just a little while I'll insert that game for *you* to try.)

When I did start writing, members of the San Dimas writers' group took parts of chapters home one Wednesday to critique, and returned them the following Wednesday. Several rewrites of each topic—the Monk, the Wife, the Cook, and all the others—were often necessary before *everyone* understood my explanation. My conscientious, friendly editors took multiple sections to work on—first rewrite, second or third rewrite—each part clearly labeled to keep things organized.

First came getting to know the Pilgrims, one at a time (emptying one cigar box at a time). Not until the zodiac and the planets were all accounted for did I know how extensive the introductory chapter had to be, and what subjects it had to cover. After all of the basic personalities were recognized, considerable thought had to be given to the Pilgrims "leftover." These "unknowns" demanded scrutiny. How do you penetrate Chaucer's creative thinking beyond the obvious, the expected? The answer is, be faithful to his clues.

The answer to one question astonished me. The Manciple is the only Pilgrim with no physical description whatever. It makes sense to match him with Libra, the Scales, which is the only inanimate zodiac figure. A manciple is a purchasing agent. Knowing, from pictures, that scales were used in business transactions in the Middle Ages, I tried to make a firm connection that way. After a good deal of time and effort I discovered, quite serendipitously, that the word *Libra*, itself, signifies *pound*. That's why the symbol for the British pound is a peculiar L—£. Libra *directly* signifies money which *is* our primary purchasing agent! Chaucer guides your steps once you start dancing to his tune.

Another question confounded me: How can a crab have a tail? When Chaucer presents a picture of Cancer, the Crab, he depicts females with something trailing behind. That made no sense until a book of cathedral carvings showed me that *lobster* as well as *crab* can be expressed, in Latin, by the word *cancer*. And I got another bonus (like the quiver and arrows) from that cathedral photo book. On the page next to Cancer, I found a representation of Jupiter (pagan god *and* planet) as a plump *monk*. After that, I would seek and find many more instances of Christian images in the form of pagan personalities. The merging of Christian with pagan concepts fits the developing pilgrim plan.

An amusing character is the flighty Pilgrim Canon. He rushes in, travels with the Pilgrims for a short time and then suddenly rushes away again. With a mindset on celestial figures, it is easy to see him as a comet—appearing among the stars, abiding a while, and then disappearing. Chaucer's details to prove this are fun to discover.

A horrifying moment, that still makes me shudder, came when I recognized the Pilgrim Pardoner as Pisces, the Sign of the Fish. Another meaning of "the sign of the fish" is the Church. The Pardoner's role, as the one who grants pardon, becomes a solid connection. Chaucer depicts him as abhorrent. The Pardoner preys upon the poor. I have no desire to say more—but Chaucer does.

When a few individuals who have eluded discovery are left, you turn to the process of elimination. Be forewarned that prejudice—prejudging who a Pilgrim *has* to be—mustn't cloud your vision. Take only Chaucer's words as your guide. As a case in point, there are few women among the Pilgrims—only three. Among the zodiac and planets there are few "women"—only three: Venus, Virgo, and the Moon. They must match the Prioress, her shadowy companion, and the Wife of Bath.

Let's first look at Venus. The motto "Love conquers all" surely indicates Venus, the goddess of love. The fact that the Pilgrim with this motto is a nun must not shake our faith in Chaucer's words. We learned, a short time ago, that gods and goddesses were illustrated as Christian figures (Jupiter as a monk, for example). Her title, as prioress, means she ranks first. Venus, as the morning star, is the singular beauty among the planets.

Our next female Pilgrim is the Wife of Bath. Let's toss a mental coin and test her clues against Virgo, instead of the Moon. Remember not to prejudge the lady because she is a wife. How could she be the virgin Virgo? To begin with, there is a goddess (one of those associated with Virgo) who renews her virginity every year by means of *a bath*. That's why Chaucer's Wife *comes from Bath!* One other solid clue Chaucer gives is the lady wears spurs. It might seem odd that she is the *only* Pilgrim with spurs. That is meant to be noticeable. It's not odd at all, but relatively expected when Virgo's most distinguishing star is a *spike*, Spica.

Now, by default, the Prioress' companion, who is generally called the Second Nun, is the Moon. Chaucer includes her as a Pilgrim although she is not seen or described, as if playing the part of the Moon on a moonless night.

How could I help but stay fascinated? Chaucer is playing a dangerous game. He is not straightforward. He couldn't afford to be. Believe in Chaucer's creativity. The clues are there—if you're patient and serious about finding them.

The second book, *Pilgrim Chaucer,* went to press in early July 1999. The press release asked, "So you thought Chaucer was bawdy? How bawdy?" Appealing to the poet's academic audience, readers were reminded of high-school days when the "good parts" of the *Canterbury Tales* (the *Miller's Tale,* for example) were sought out for "a good snicker." It then goes on to correct the reputation of *Sir Thopas*—not a "dull" story at all, but "X-rated." Books one and two confirm "that Geoffrey Chaucer was both a bawdy and religious writer, and he is an enduring master in both departments."

With *Pilgrim Chaucer* in its final stage of publication, the time had come to tantalize John Daniel with the game that would introduce book three. He knew nothing of all the activity that had occupied my friends and me all these months. But before I could approach him with a new idea, the book had to have a name. I toyed with several titles that were subtle, ordinary. I finally told myself I had to have the courage to say exactly what the book contained, no beating about the bush. I must not be swayed by the general prejudice against allegory. Book three would be called "Chaucer's Pilgrims: the Allegory." I sent off the puzzle without the solution as a way of demonstrating my confidence in how clear

Chaucer's pictures are. And, by not including the solution, it also said I had confidence in John's sleuthing ability. (I would not be disappointed.)

Now, with the all-important letter on its way to John, I spent part of a day designing a shirt to celebrate the publication of book two. The first T-shirt had been fun. This second one would have the little grotesque of the *Pilgrim Chaucer* cover on the front of the shirt, and a somewhat cryptic message on the back.

The
Chaucer
anniversary
is coming.

Already excited about next year's anniversary, it seemed just right.

John's reply to the puzzle arrived on July 26. He explained that it took a while to answer, not because he had been slow to "get it," but because correspondence had been piled high.

> Thanks for the teaser on *Chaucer's Pilgrims: the Allegory*. It appears you've found a whole zodiac of characters in *The Canterbury Tales*. How fascinating! What fun it must have been to solve the puzzle. To even see the puzzle, let alone solve it. So yes, I'd love to see more. I'm eager to find out how water-tight this interpretation of yours is.

He closed with best wishes.

His interest couldn't help but be inspiring. The calendar also inspired me. October 1999, the date I was working toward, was now only eight weeks away. That book dream had a good chance of coming true, but the manuscript John eagerly anticipated had not been completed! My search for facts, photos, and fantasies still occupied each day—and night.

There were several hurdles yet to clear. I had seen some of them from a long way off: wondering who the Clerk might be, and the yeomen I mentioned, for instance. Then there is the number

29. It surely has a deep significance. Why else would the Host (in the prelude to the final tale) address the 29 Pilgrims, referring to their social status as *degrees*, and in addition allude to "nine and twenty" degrees in celestial terms? That connection eluded me until the very moment I needed it. And, after mulling over the zodiac figures for a sufficient amount of time, it amused me when I suddenly understood why some of the Pilgrims tell no stories, are *never* heard from. (Patience! I'll let you in on that in a little while.) But, while some hurdles had been cleared, a completely unexpected and insurmountable obstacle arose directly in my path with no way of getting around it.

On a very warm August afternoon, I made a list of all the loose ends that needed to be connected. With nothing more than the intention of being neat and tidy, of verifying every detail, an apparently trivial gesture on my part brought years of mental activity to a jolting standstill. To be "thorough," I looked at a map to verify the comparative locations of London, where the Pilgrims begin their journey, and Canterbury, their destination. Having already established that they are stars and planets, they appear to be moving, we know from simple observation, east to west. Can you imagine my utter confusion, my downright panic, when the map showed that London to Canterbury indicates the reverse—west to east?

The book that guides the ethics and practicality of my research says if you find that your thesis cannot be supported, it must be dropped *immediately*. I believe that. I would act accordingly. At the moment of the west to east discovery, however, I couldn't *drop* it. I was frozen, unable to move. I had come a long way; a great number of ideas fit into place; the developing pattern was a splendid creation. How could it all come apart, fall in a meaningless heap, at this late date? While part of my mind remained frozen, another part began to repeat over and over, louder and louder—*there is something you do not know!*

All preceding research became inoperative while I made an urgent trip to Honnold in the cool morning of the following day. I checked out several books written by ancient authors, about stars and the way the heavens were believed to operate. By the end of the day, reading one authority after another, I found the information I had lacked. Because the zodiac does not behave quite as smoothly as the early stargazers felt it could, they proposed (and believed) that a force they named the Prime Mover caused the stars to lag against their natural tendency. That is the ingenious explanation for why the signs do not come around in exactly twelve months, and, therefore, why the calendar has needed to be realigned several times over the centuries. So, that meant the Pilgrims, slowly, ever so slowly, were actually tending *west to east*—no matter what our eyes tell us about the sky in one night. I breathed a grand sigh of relief as the giant obstacle disappeared. This knowledge would also add meaning to my later interpretations.

Now for the challenge of the Clerk and yeomen. The way to understand the part the yeomen play is connected to the Pilgrims they travel with, and gets a bit unwieldy to explain here. I'll just say they function with what the Pilgrim they serve represents. (See *Chaucer's Pilgrims* for the complete explanation.)

The Clerk is not quite as complicated. After the twelve constellations and the planets had all been accounted for, a lone Pilgrim remained. Why would Chaucer include an extraneous personality? Partly, I believe, to make things more intricate, not as easy to solve. Early Romans and others had a belief, still prevalent when Chaucer lived, which envisioned worthy souls transported to the heavens when they died. (That's part of Chaucer's creative imagination for himself as Pilgrim Chaucer; he portrays himself as one of those who will be among the stars.) How do we decipher the clues about this Clerk? First of all, stories the Pilgrims tell help us to identify them. The claim, here, is that Petrarch "taught" the Pilgrim Clerk his story. Because of this, we will assume Petrarch *is* the Clerk, and search for Chaucer's identifiers to confirm this.

Petrarch had died ten years before the *Canterbury Tales* were begun. Never had there been an influence in Europe so rapid, powerful and far-reaching as the humanist thinking recorded in his many writings. And beyond humanism, he aided the reconciliation of the classical (pagan) world with medieval Christianity. (The dual identities of Chaucer's Pilgrims can be seen as examples of this reconciliation.) That influence alone would make him deserving of being transported to the stars, but there is more. Chaucer says of this Pilgrim Clerk: Gladly would he learn and gladly teach. This Clerk, we are told, is more interested in learning and books than in money or entertainment, an opinion held about Petrarch by his contemporaries. And, finally, there is the Pilgrim Clerk's physical description: lean as a rake, not fat, but hollow and serious, or solemn. *Hollow* is strange. What kind of man is hollow? I see a grim-faced skeleton, the "threadbare" garment he is said to wear holds the image of a shroud. Chaucer has honored the dead writer by placing his spirit among the stars. This identification is an educated guess that fits the clues.

The next question is, why do some of the pilgrims tell no stories? It became clear to me that the guiding force of the *Tales* is not the surface stories, nor surface identities, but the covert, celestial characteristics. That gives the zodiac figures each a *single* personality, no matter how many Pilgrims are included to play the part of the sign. Then we expect the *two* brothers, who are Gemini, to have only one story. (The Parson has a story; his brother, the Plowman, does not.) It is also why the five Guildsmen who travel with the Pilgrim Cook—the six characters together portray the figure of Cancer—have no narratives. (The Cook tells a story; the five Guildsmen never say a word.)

And, as a final hurdle, let's look at Chaucer's odd number. Recognizing the stellar and planetary aspect as the guiding force is part of what makes the number 29 so significant. The San Dimas writers often joked about *29*, asking if I'd figured it out yet. No. Only when I had nothing more to think about than the last introduction could I perceive the pilgrimage from an ordinary point of view, disassociated from astrology. The Parson is the last Pilgrim to tell a tale. His offering amounts to a traditional and thorough examination of conscience. The Host speaks a prelude to the Pilgrim Parson's entrance, and makes two seemingly flagrant "errors" regarding the heavens. Is there a better way for Chaucer to attract attention? Sorting out his trickery has many facets, but I think the following will provide enough understanding.

First, remember the Middle Ages pictured time as a circle. They also referred to a *Great Year*, the period of time it would take for all the stars to return to the precise locations they had had when time began. At the end of that Great Year—when the circling movement of stars and planets is complete—time would run out. The world would end. The *Canterbury Tales* were being written in the last two decades of the fourteenth century; many believed and calculated the end of the world to be at hand. For the Host to tell the Pilgrims that he is reading the sun to be at 29 degrees—each sign has 30 degrees—it indicates that when his calculation reaches 30 degrees the world will end.

Chaucer also reflects the same thinking as he tells us, in this same prelude, that the Pilgrims have nearly reached the end of their travels. (The heavenly bodies are almost back in the portentous initial arrangement.) The group is urged to make haste. The mention of Libra, the Scales, an image of justice, denotes that the time of Judgment is near. There is more, but I think that will suffice.

I haven't said much about them lately, but always, every week, the San Dimas writers continued their critiquing and advising—catching typos, questioning verb tenses, declaring an explanation confusing. Getting the book in good order would have been impossible without them. And you can be sure they all cheered the answer to *29*.

On September 8, 1999, a couple of weeks short of the deadline, I sent the completed manuscript by certified mail. (For good measure, I included the oft rejected bee story—the *Cook's Tale*—as an appendix. It had so patiently waited to see the world.) Even though I had given John early notice that many more characters would be dealt with in book three, he exclaimed, "This is a whopper!" but followed with, "I'm sure the length is justified." I couldn't help smile at his vote of confidence. Then we all waited to see if John found it properly "water-tight."

Ten days later, John called to offer a contract for *Chaucer's Pilgrims*. The manuscript held water. He congratulated me on completing the trilogy; that dream from 1972 would soon become a complete reality.

With the contract for book three came a letter that said I could expect the second book, *Pilgrim Chaucer*, any day. Susan had distributed examination copies as she had with *Chaucer's Host*. When I received my little box of ten copies, John's accompanying letter referred to my ideas as "important and entertaining." What a lift. *Library Journal*, Oct 15, 1999 published the first review of the second book, *Pilgrim Chaucer*.

> Cullen's method of explication is conventional.... But some critics would consider the precise meaning she finds unconventional.... Overall, though, Cullen's approach is scholarly and her interpretation supported by extensive notes. Recommended for academic libraries supporting studies in medieval literature.

I had a different approach, but it appeared to be appreciated.

The three books about Chaucer's hidden message were soon to be part of the literary world. I realized I must get ready to step out into the world myself. Feelings of inadequacy, in relation to professors I'd had dealings with, had to be overcome. Gathering all my courage, I determined to start with planned visits to local Chaucer professors and offer them copies of *Chaucer's Host* and *Pilgrim Chaucer*. The academic I would call on first would be Dr. Elliott, my long-time-ago Chaucer professor.

Up until now I'd had a tidy little life, attending the San Dimas writers' group, visiting Virginia, and spending as much time as I wanted at the Honnold Library. But for the next twelve months life became more of a three-ring circus. And before I could take time to chat with professors, a critical issue had to be resolved.

In September John had said he looked forward "to being the proud publisher of *Chaucer's Pilgrims*," but by mid-October concerns had developed about my desire to maintain "secrecy," to heighten the surprise for the reader. If I wanted to keep the *secret*

[120] Ensnared by His Words

of the double identities, what could John say on the back cover to tempt the browsing potential book buyer? What could a press release say that would stimulate interest?

Posing the question to Judy Wenrick, she offered to have me put the situation before her Advanced Placement Language Arts students at Upland High School. What a memorable afternoon! I gave the students a little background about how the Pilgrims' double identities came to me in a flash. Then I handed out printed copies of the game I had made up. They each read as I spoke. Here is the game so you can test *your* deciphering skills.

All the pilgrims (with their dual personalities) arrive at sunset. Chaucer saw them—and so have you, or there would be no point to the game.

To begin with, let's note:
    There are *no children.*
    There are *no married couples.*
    The group is *almost all men* (only three women).
    One pilgrim has *no physical description*, is identified by a
        function—*purchasing agent.*

We'll begin with the most energetic character who has
    broad shoulders
    wide, black nostrils
    and could knock a door off its hinges by running into it
        with his head.

There is
    one pair of brothers.

There is also a slender journeyer who
    is easily angered
    has long, extremely thin legs
    is as dreaded as death
    and lives in the shadows on uncultivated land.

There is a man who calls for *water*.

Another man appears to ride *very high on a horse*.

The Host is especially solicitous toward two others
   a man dedicated to war
   and a woman whose motto is "love conquers all."
They, too, arrive as part of the group and also remain for the night.

There are many other personalities for a total of 29. I have chosen just the ones most easily visualized.
   Small hint: All the figures, loosely speaking, are an organized group that arrives at sunset and stays all night.
   Bigger hint: Concentrate on forming a picture of the door-smasher. Almost every successful sleuth begins there.

When the game ended, there was total silence. Judy prompted her class, "Don't be shy. Do you see an image or have an idea?"
   A young man directly in front of me stated matter-of-factly, "They're stars, of course." A young lady followed immediately with, "The door-smasher must be a bull." She hardly had the words out when she exclaimed, "Taurus!" After that, answers and ideas came from all directions, like corn popping. Gemini! Scorpio! Aquarius! Sagittarius! Mars! Venus! I don't know who had more fun—the students or me. They even identified the pilgrim with no physical description—inanimate Libra, the Scales. When the flurry of excitement tapered off, I brought up the question John had asked. What can be said on the cover if I want to keep the secret? A consensus held that a general idea *had* to be divulged—but no details. The details, they all judged, would be entertaining enough while reading the book.
   When the students handed back the printed game sheets, there were remarks written along the edges. One said, "This was sooo suspenseful! It's the first time I've been on the edge of my

seat reading something." Another said, "I feel as if I've walked into a whole new world." There were many other comments. Those pages are a precious keepsake, and the excitement the game created a treasured memory.

Taking the judgment of the students seriously, I rewrote the introduction and told John he could present the basic idea to the public.

VII.

The 600th Year

With the answer to the "secrecy" dilemma worked out, the following week I got around to calling the English Department at Cal Poly to inquire about Dr. Elliott's office hours. I picked a convenient time in the early afternoon and took a bus to the campus. I sat waiting outside his office, gathering my confidence. He recognized me even with my gray hair. "I'll be happy to chat for a while," he said, "but there are things I planned to do before my next class, an hour from now."

I assured him I would only stay a short time. For my first such venture, I planned being there just long enough to offer him my books and wish him well. (I had heard that he'd been ill. I didn't want to cause him stress.) He took the books and set them aside. Chaucer, he said, would not be on the class schedule for the year. That disappointed me greatly. We spoke of teachers I knew and then of more personal matters about religion. He and I belonged to the same parish. He had been invited to participate in a religious conference in February, a few months hence, but hadn't made up his mind whether or not to attend. The more he told me about the conference, the more I encouraged him to take part in it.

We talked on and on, as if time were of no importance. At last he looked at the clock and said his class started in ten minutes. We stood up to leave his office, but our conversation had not ended! We continued to chat as we walked to the adjoining building. When we reached the doorway, I extended my hand. He took it momentarily and said, "Maybe I was wrong." With those final words, he turned and entered the building. As I strolled across the campus, heading toward the bus for home, I mulled over the meaning of his parting words. Could he be questioning his attitude toward my ideas? I couldn't be sure. Perhaps he felt that thirty years before he should have encouraged me. I've thought about it often, but have never been certain. Dr. Elliott retired a short time later. I never saw him again.

That first interview, which I approached with apprehension, turned out very differently from what I'd imagined. It gave me a foretaste of a year of events I could not have conceived or anticipated.

A few days later I called the English Departments at both Scripps College and Pomona College here in Claremont. In each case, I inquired of the department secretary the name of the professor who taught Chaucer. Each secretary hesitated. (I soon understood the hesitation.) Rephrasing my question, I asked who would teach medieval literature. That gave me the necessary information, the name and office hour. Each professor received me pleasantly and accepted the books I offered. One professor, when the subject turned to Chaucer, told me he covered Chaucer in the first week of a survey course. The second man explained that his course, called "Chaucer and Medieval London," had a sociological as well as historical emphasis. Both professors claimed that, if a course consisting only of Chaucer's writings were offered, no one would sign up. I expressed amazement, saying, "I thought Chaucer would be required!" Both professors insisted their college programs were more *flexible*.

Flexibility is not what I saw, nor would Virginia. The time had come to report my findings to her. I had visited professors to gain courage, and in addition gained a sad up-to-date picture of the local world of Chaucer studies.

"What is happening to the teaching of literature?" Virginia fumed. That is when the contest idea was born to stir up interest, to draw attention to Chaucer. In a few weeks it would be his 600th anniversary year. That made for good timing.

Early in December 1999, I received the first proof pages for book three, *Chaucer's Pilgrims*. The pages did not need to be returned before mid-January, so I felt I could devote some time to this contest project before getting to work on the proofing.

I searched reference books at Honnold, found a listing for the "New Chaucer Society" and sent them a letter about the contest Virginia had proposed. The holidays and the December school break delayed our receiving a reply from the secretary of the Chaucer Society until mid-January 2000. My entire year-end writing schedule cleared just as a serious problem arose where none had been foreseen.

The problem had to do with Dr. Barnes. Though retired in 1998, as the Chaucer professor at Pomona College, he maintained an office near the campus. In spring of 1999, I chanced to meet him in town. When he asked about Chaucer, I told him of *Pilgrim Chaucer* on the verge of entering the world, and about book three now in progress. He said he'd enjoy seeing book three. So, in June, when a good portion of the text (but without footnotes) looked passable, I dropped off 200 pages for him to read. I gladly gave him a portion of the manuscript, but didn't count on his being able to review it because he was not well.

With the many things that occupied my mind and my time, I actually gave Dr. Barnes little thought. Now, early in December 1999, a phone call from him surprised me. "I've had your manuscript quite a while, but I *have* finished looking it over. Would you like to pick it up at my home?" Recovering from my surprise, I said I'd be there Saturday afternoon.

Dr. Barnes answered the door. We talked for a short time while he sat in an easy chair. It pleased him that someone (meaning me) would actively be working with the *Canterbury Tales*. "A strong force in academia," he confided, "is attempting to have all literature before Shakespeare removed from the standard curriculum." He knew the college world; it worried him that appreciation of early literature had diminished. And what a sad revelation for me! That news fit what I had recently experienced. There were more and more things to think about.

When I got home I examined the pages he had read. Most were unmarked. Here and there he recommended a better or additional word—specify "temple" instead of "structure," for example. Two of my examples, he felt, were weak; the evidence given, inadequate. In one instance, I simply claimed "official approval" for a goddess called *the Great Mother*. Concrete statements regarding her elevated position would have to be included, such as, the Palatine temple built in her honor and coins struck with her image. That would justify the claim of "official" acceptance.

I knew these changes would inevitably create that situation for Eric which I had been so carefully instructed to avoid. I contemplated each of Dr. Barnes' criticisms. Substitutions for three words appeared necessary, beneficial. The paragraphs involved would probably maintain their contours. I also decided that one or two sentences must be added on several pages. Those additions, without doubt, would cause the text to need adjustment—and also the subsequent pages.

I gave scrupulous attention to printing out the insertions, attached them to the pages involved, and highlighted where revisions were to be entered. That process, along with proofing the 425 pages I had received from Fithian Press, took many days. The fateful time of Y2K engulfed the world, when one millennium terminated and we entered another. In spite of all the hubbub that caused, I hardly took notice of it.

I returned the pages, including the formidable changes, the first week of January 2000—then braced myself for Eric's reaction. On January 18, his reply arrived. It had taken him several days to absorb the shock. The protest I expected was there, but tempered with his understanding of my position.

> I've received your page proofs of Chaucer's Pilgrims. To tell you the truth, I received them a week ago, but was so horrified I waited until now to write.... Let me say, for the record: Bad, bad, bad author! As you know, this is exactly the kind of thing I hoped to avoid when we discussed it some months ago.... I do understand, however, how important Dr. Barnes's comments are to you, and that we must consider them. It would be a big mistake not to.
>
> I should tell you that there will probably be some charge to you for revision, after I've made these changes.

It may also force us to set the schedule back a few weeks, but not enough to make a big difference.

The situation I had caused would be manageable. The letter ended on a positive note. "The way you've indicated the changes is fine, and I'll have no trouble following it." What a relief to have it settled.

I wrote a note of acceptance and appreciation.

> Scolding acknowledged. I'm sure you realize the "Barnes" changes were not made to aggravate you, nor were they made because I didn't understand our "little talk." After due consideration, I felt that if I'm not going to make the best presentation I can, what's the point of what I'm doing?
> What's gotta be, 'zgotta be. I'm sure you'll be fair.

With the give-and-take accomplished, Eric and I returned to our easy-going relationship. When the revising had been done, and the time involved tallied, the cost of the extra hours would be calculated.

In the meantime, the much-looked-for response from the New Chaucer Society (NCS) came at last. They agreed to sponsor the competition, dependent upon the approval of their Board of Trustees; that approval followed in early February. NCS would announce the competition, receive the entries, judge them, and award the prize. Virginia and I each contributed half the prize money, fittingly a total of $600 in this 600th anniversary year.

The secretary of NCS asked if I had an email address for more efficient communication. I didn't, of course, but when I mentioned this to Virginia, her friend Connie was with her. Connie took the phone to insist, "Dolores, if you are in research, you *must* avail yourself of the internet."

My professed disinterest had only been a delaying tactic. With that word of wisdom, early in February, I ventured into the realm of *www*. (Asked to compose a screen name—at this moment in

Chaucer history—the natural choice seemed to be "Chaucer600," and so it is.) What a world of information! My first email told John Daniel that I had courageously plunged into this pool of communication. I closed with, "I would be happy to get a reply when I log on (is that properly said?) next time." Isn't that unbelievably formal? John congratulated me. I soon loosened up. Email became more conversation than stiff letter-writing.

Dealing with something of consequence, however, still enlists the U.S. Postal Service. To wit, the letter that arrived from John on March 10 detailed the extra hours of labor poured into the proof pages.

> Eric estimates that your alterations necessitated 16 hours of work...it has also delayed the schedule by a couple of weeks. I'm afraid I'll have to charge you. Because I want you to know that we're as anxious as you are to have this book correct in all respects, I'll lower that total [by one fourth].
>
> Other than that, Eric tells me the book's progressing nicely.

John had the final word about business. I thought it fair and considerate. I have often said—and for good reason—John is a *mensch*.

In the last week of March the much-labored-over second proof pages were delivered to me. Eric urged that I take special note of the areas that had been altered and—very important—check the internal references to page numbers. If a statement had originally indicated "see p. 125 above," is the connection still *p. 125*, or had it shifted to *p. 126?* Hours of patience, concentration, and devotion followed. This would be my last chance to present my case.

While proofing, I received a pleasant and exciting distraction—the NCS spring newsletter. Announcement of the competition made the front page. Submissions must answer the question, "Why, after 600 years, are we still studying the works of

Chaucer?" and be limited to one page (500 words). Both scholars and students were encouraged to participate as Virginia and I had wished. I read the entire article to Virginia. We were confident that good would come from our plan.

As I said earlier, the year became a three-ring circus. NCS occupied one ring, the internet another. But the main attraction, in the center ring, continued to be preparing book three, *Chaucer's Pilgrims*, to go to press. The first week of April, by U.S. mail, I received the cover design for approval. John had created a parade of silhouettes in single file, as an impression of the pilgrims. Being both publisher and artist, he made an amusing Freudian slip; the characters, he said, were arranged "from left to write." In any case, because they resembled rural images from 1900 more than medieval travelers, I said I'd send him figures that were more appropriate. After a bit of back-and-forth, we combined Chaucer's themes from astronomy and astrology by using an event called the conjunction (coming together) of Venus and Mars, incorporating a medieval, a celestial, and a dual image in one illustration. *Chaucer's Pilgrims* would head for the printer July 1.

At my next visit to Virginia, she suggested I contact the Claremont city library about having a book signing. On my walk home, I dropped in to talk with Mr. Charles Kaufman, the library manager. He seemed tentative about the idea, but not negative. Two more visits finally got him to pencil in October 17. It would be advantageous for our celebration to have my appearance at the library prior to October 25. The day of the actual anniversary turned out to be a story in itself. It's a good story with happy details I'll share in just a bit.

Previous thoughts of anticipated events have intervened, but we're really talking, at the moment, about several weeks in May when I searched the internet for Chaucer buffs by finding homepages that included the name "Chaucer." Two of those early contacts have become friends. One—Adrienne Allen—an eighth grader then, and a multitalented writer and musician, is now about to graduate from Brown University. The second friend is Dr. Candace Rodman (a.k.a. *Prioresse*) of Indiana, a professor in the field of English as a Second Language. Candace is devoted to Hildegard of Bingen in particular, and the Middle Ages in general.

Perusing the copy of that NCS newsletter beyond the front page, I found there were Chaucer lovers all over the world. What a promising discovery! I joined NCS immediately. Their membership list of names and email addresses put me in touch with hundreds of people who take Chaucer seriously. I contacted a few to say "Hi, I'm new here," and offer the riddle game. Some were takers. Some, not surprisingly, were bound by tradition; the game made them uncomfortable.

Each evening I'd e-contact several NCS members, and respond to those who had gotten in touch with me, since I last logged on. What fun! Emails arrived from Hawaii, Japan, Turkey, Spain, France, England, and Canada. That would surely stimulate conversation at the international NCS conference in July. Up until now the game had been a small, local endeavor. Now, in one month's time, by email, it had circled the globe.

I generally made a report to Virginia each week. This sudden burst of activity astonished her. Having lost her sight before computers became household items, such capabilities were mysterious and overwhelming to her. Attempting to explain, I compared the speed and distance to phone messages, with the result printed on a TV screen. She looked deep in thought. Then her face brightened. She said, "There is no stopping your new idea now."

I would share special messages I received with her, like the charming words of encouragement from Professor Hamaguchi in Japan. "The 'riddle' is the best way," he said, "in attracting the curiosity of students and general readers. Then, Chaucer becomes the exciting topic for classes. It's like 'games of dragon quest' on computer or exciting detective novels."

A professor from Cambridge, England who reviewed the game apologized with, "I'm sorry to throw cold water on your enthusiasm." Not a bit discouraged, I sent him a frank reply.

Dear Professor Brewer:
The event I describe, the sudden identifications, is not

meant to be entertainment. It is just what happened to me. With such insight, one can hardly ignore the possibilities. It has been a challenging search for the proper evidence. Your words do not act as cold water because you have no idea how intense my enthusiasm is. Many have said similar words. There is no turning back, no denying what I see. The book, *Chaucer's Pilgrims*, will be published before the October anniversary. That fulfills one of my dearest wishes.

He answered diplomatically.

Dear Ms Cullen:
Congratulations on sticking to your guns. You will go far. Your work will certainly arouse interest.
    Yours sincerely,
    Derek Brewer

While I spent time becoming better acquainted with the internet, Fithian Press put the finishing touches on *Chaucer's Pilgrims*. It went to the printer on July 1, bearing my official acknowledgement, "In appreciation of The Libraries of the Claremont Colleges—my home away from home." The spotlight in the center ring of the circus went dark.

On July 14, the NCS Congress assembled in London. The name of the winner of the competition became history—Robert Meyer-Lee, a graduate student at Yale. Virginia and I could not have been more pleased. His essay captured the fascination of Chaucer's elusive spirit. The awarding of the prize concluded the activity in the NCS ring of the circus. That cleared the way for directing all attention to the grand finale, the day of the 600th anniversary itself—only three months away.

I had been thinking about the approaching centenary long before the possibility of book three took shape. In 1998, I occasionally mailed letters to centers of Chaucer interest to ask what sort of observance they planned. Canterbury Cathedral said "there are plans being formed" and added that the University of Kent was "considering some academic event." Westminster Abbey knew that NCS planned something, "perhaps an Evensong" during July 2000, but that's all they knew. The Huntington Library here in California, hub of Chaucer scholarship in the U.S., said they had "scheduled a Chaucer exhibit for the fall of 2000," which would display their "rich collection of manuscripts and early printed books." That had great potential. They also raised the hope that there "will be similar efforts across the Atlantic."

In December of 1999, I wrote the U.S. Postal Service Stamp Development Office, the people in charge of designing new stamps, to suggest that a sheet of the Canterbury Pilgrims would be a splendid idea for October 2000. Unfortunately, my suggestion came too late to be implemented. The process for getting a stamp ready for sale takes two to three years. (I still think it's a good idea and may write to them again.)

As the year 2000 drew near, I made more serious inquiries. I wanted to know how the Chaucer world planned to celebrate, so I'd have an opportunity to consider how I could participate. I wrote to well-known journals and groups I was aware of, to ask about intentions of commemorating the auspicious occasion. The outcome of all the correspondence confirmed Dr. Barnes' somber insight.

The Center for Medieval and Renaissance Studies knew of only one Chaucer item, a lecture, to be given at a conference in December 1999, not as part of a celebration at all. *Medium Ævum*, published by the Society for Study of Medieval Language and Literature, had nothing commemorative in the works, nor did *Speculum* (Medieval Academy of America). The Association of Literary Scholars and Critics said "unfortunately" they had no plans. The International English Honor Society (*Sigma Tau Delta*) gave a small flicker of hope. They would discuss the idea of a specific remembrance at their Board Meeting in March 2000. The Early English Text Society had not scheduled the production of a distinctive Middle English volume of Chaucer for this once in a century occasion!

I could hardly believe the lack of interest or enthusiasm among academics who—I had imagined—would be eager to draw attention to the first genius of the English language. The NCS evening at Westminster Abbey in July, and Canterbury Cathedral event in October, it appeared, would be the extent of British festivity.

If the Evensong would be the only newsworthy event, I wanted to collect all the coverage and pictures I could find, as a remembrance. To that end, after the NCS ceremony in the Abbey had taken place, I visited the Honnold Library to scan the *London Times*. I could find no mention, not a line, about the ritual dedicated to Chaucer. I emailed an inquiry to the NCS secretary. She said she had seen no reporters there. I wrote to the *Times* to scold, and recommended they could make amends by doing a particular article in October for the actual date.

Then I emailed Professor Derek Brewer, drawing attention to the lack of notice in the *Times*, "It is beyond my belief that England, that London, would fail to find Chaucer's (anniversary) commemoration newsworthy. I am at a loss to understand."

His response lamented at length the British lack of interest, then tossed the ball into our court. "Clearly we must rely on the modern equivalent of the U.S. Cavalry to come to our rescue, as seems to be happening with the NCS itself and such efforts as your own."

Recalling Dr. Barnes' words about the cooling trend toward the age of Chaucer, I found the whole thing alarming. If the rest of the world seemed ready to bypass the red-letter day, then those of us in Claremont would manage our own celebration. But what to do? Where to begin?

Among Catholics, it is customary to have a Mass said on the anniversary of a death. That would also have been true when Chaucer lived. My friend Barbara reminded me that Chaucer's last sentiment was, in fact, a request for prayer. The closing of the *Canterbury Tales* is a prayer that begins: "All who hear or read this, I beseech you to pray for me." A small, private Mass at my home seemed appropriate, with eight or ten Chaucer-lovers attending. Early in September 2000, I spoke with the secretary at our parish office to make arrangements for a home Mass on the evening of October 25. When the pastor, Father (now Monsignor) Tom Welbers got word that it would commemorate the date of Chaucer's death, the event shifted into public focus. The Mass would be celebrated in church; invitations would go out to all the English Departments in our area; newspapers should be notified, including *The Tidings*, the Los Angeles archdiocese publication. With unexpected, but gratifying enthusiasm, Father Tom urged, "It's a celebration that needs to be publicized."

To picture many people attending a Mass in church would require a whole new plan. Now where do we begin? Think publicity, music, food, and who knows what else. A special Mass needed special music. From many years of enjoying live performances of music from the Middle Ages and Renaissance here in Claremont, I knew just the person to call—Shirley Robbins. She directed medieval instrumental ensembles, and trained vocalists in the techniques of "early music," as it is called. My invitation got a warm reception from Shirley. "I'd be delighted to take part," she said.

With the music arranged for, next came food. The Mass would have to be followed by a reception, of course, and the menu would have to be medieval. I borrowed a book called *Pleyn Delit* from the Honnold Library. Constance Hieatt, the author, had adjusted medieval recipes for modern cooks, including well-thought-out substitutions of modern ingredients. The book did contain a great variety of "*delit*-ful" recipes.

We would plan a dinner, and we needed to think about some food-to-go for those unable to spend a whole evening. The fast-food would be black bread and cups of cheese custard. Those who had more time would have a sit-down dinner of selected recipes the like of which they may never have tasted before.

We'd begin with a salad of greens. (Tomatoes were unknown to Chaucer.) Vinegar and oil added to a combination of minced fresh parsley, sage, mint, fennel, dill, and savory create a palate-pleasing dressing. The greens would be creative—borage, spinach, and whatever else is available, along with thinly sliced small leeks and scallions. Hieatt's one caution to preserve authenticity: *avoid iceberg lettuce*. Besides the salad, we would make cheese-mushroom pasties, and pork tarts flavored with nutmeg, ginger, cardamom, pepper, and saffron. Dessert would be apple-almond pudding.

What to drink? Mead for the toast to Chaucer must be found, but what to serve as a dinner beverage? The fourteenth century had no coffee, tea, or chocolate. An email to Professor Hieatt brought a ready answer—apple cider.

Cider, in October, could be found at any grocery store. Mead, on the other hand, presented a challenge—with a happy ending. A local baker agreed to make the black bread, but said the request surprised him. As I told him about the Chaucer feast-in-the-making, a woman standing beside me interjected, "You'll have mead, of course." I said we hadn't been able to find any. Smiling like a fairy godmother, she offered, "Just give me your phone number. I'll call you when I get home and tell you the number for my local supplier." She was a woman of her word. It took only a phone call to a nearby town to order a case of, wouldn't you know, *Chaucer's* Mead.

Talking about Chaucer at the city library, a week before our medieval extravaganza, made for perfect timing. The evening could not have been more successful. Mr. Kaufman had evidently alerted local high school English teachers. Quite a number of rather stoic young students arrived. They likely were promised extra credit for attending. One young man sat in the first row, facing the lectern. He looked determined, but not cheerful. That would change.

As the crowd gathered, library helpers brought additional chairs, and then more chairs. I recognized half the faces as friends; the other half were strangers. That's about perfect, and I said so. The high point of the evening came for me, and for Mr. Kaufman, when Virginia Adair arrived and made her way to the front row.

The talk I gave mainly introduced book three, *Chaucer's Pilgrims*, which had just been published. We played the little sleuthing game, of course. And when I paused to ask if anyone understood—Did someone see an image?—the "determined" young man fairly leapt off his chair. "It's Taurus! That's the zodiac!" His energetic display got a laugh, but he proved to be a catalyst. Other people started adding more identifications. How wonderful! Many people bought the books, and had me sign them. That's another kind of thrill. At the very end of my presentation, I invited everyone to the Chaucer Mass and reception the following week.

The library event began a "Chaucer octave"—eight days devoted to his commemoration. Baking became a major part of that eight-day ritual.

In making a plan for the Chaucer evening, it would not be proper for me to leave the Mass early to attend to the food and beverages, so I asked Judy Wenrick and her husband Jon, who had often extended a helping Chaucer hand, if they would oversee the dining activities in the hall. Always obliging, they agreed to be part of the grand finale. Judy had the last word about serving the food, and the seating arrangements. Jon took responsibility for opening and pouring the mead—and proposing a Chaucer toast.

Email invitations were sent to English departments in the area. The Curator of Manuscripts at the Huntington Library planned to attend. People of the parish came. San Dimas writers came, including Pat Sheehan, who has since published her Irish memoir; she assisted with serving the meal.

With the Mass about to begin, I welcomed the guests seated in the church with Chaucer's prayer request in Middle English—followed by the same words in today's English. That signaled the recorder players and the percussionist, with his little drum, to lead the altar servers and Father Tom, the celebrant, down the aisle. From the first thump on the drum, a medieval atmosphere filled the church. Shirley directed a small consort of instruments and a vocalist. When Mass ended, many of those in attendance lingered to hear the musicians' final offering. Folks short on time picked up a serving of bread and custard from a table outside the exit to the parking lot.

Most of the crowd, however, headed for the long tables set up in the parish hall. Close to one hundred attended. The food was unusual but delicious. The salad was superb. The mead was exquisite—as Virginia's poetry would soon express. When the guests asked if we would be doing this again next year, the answer would be "Yes." What a great way to give life to Chaucer's name.

As an annual affair there is one limiting stipulation. At subsequent receptions, we serve only black bread, cheese, pasties, cider and mead—no salad or pork tarts or custard or apple pudding. The elaborate menu of the 600th year will not be repeated again until the 700th year.

A few weeks later, the first review of *Chaucer's Pilgrims* arrived. *Midwest Book Review* (December 2000) called it "a fun examination of Chaucer, providing a fresh new look at Chaucer's intentions," and "a 'must' for serious readers of Chaucer." That put the icing on the anniversary cake.

VIII.

Reactions

Everything I wanted to say about the travelers in the *Canterbury Tales* had been said. The dream about the three books had come true. Many people had discovered a different and fascinating way of reading Chaucer, and I had often had the pleasure of participating first-hand in their initial thrill. Playing the game, first with family and close friends, then with the San Dimas writers, then Judy Wenrick's students, and out into the world of book stores and libraries, church groups and the internet, has filled me with memories galore.

Journals that provide recommendations for libraries had had kind words and had heartily recommended the books. With my early confusion and lack of ability (lo, these many years ago), it warms my heart to read comments like—she writes well, making difficult ideas accessible to beginners and sharing her excitement about Chaucer. To be so perceived is exactly what I *would* have wanted, all I *could* have wanted.

What I assert about Chaucer and his Pilgrims is NOT meant to discard, negate, or replace what has been claimed in the past. Chaucer's genius can accommodate numerous explications. What I describe is *an additional level of meaning*. The books deliver a new dimension of the Pilgrims as an all-encompassing overlay of time and the universe.

My experience has proven that those with a good deal of prior knowledge about Chaucer are often limited in their ability to see these dual figures. There is a cloud, a mass of information, that gets in the way of an unexpected idea. This lack of vision can be exhibited as indifference, or suspicion, or dedication to immutability.

Pursuit of the explanation for those double images, that I saw right from the start, has been absorbing, and a constant source of astonishment for me. Because of my reaction, it amazes and confuses me when it is not the same for others. A case in point is a Texas astronomer who played the sleuthing game by U.S. mail. It would be easy, you might even say automatic, that he would know the zodiac to be the answer. He did. Actually, he said he understood *before* he opened the envelope I'd mailed him, but now comes the amazing part. This new, totally different picture of the Pilgrims held no particular significance for him, did not pique his curiosity. He simply said he knew the answer, then went on to ask questions by email regarding astronomy which had nothing to do with the Pilgrims. That was that. I am nonplussed.

And there is the Pomona College faculty member, a good friend of Virginia's, who played the game when I spoke at Borders Books. After someone recognized Taurus, the professor immediately identified the two brother Pilgrims as "Gemini, the Twins." Beyond that, his interest failed. If a door opens into a previously unknown world, how can you ignore what is inside without even a look-see? I shake my head in dismay.

My unorthodox ideas and chatty style are sometimes unacceptable. A woman from Oxford, devoted to Chaucer studies, considers my interpretation too overly ingenious to accept. She says she doesn't want to caricature my analysis—which she already had—and warns devotees of allegory to be wary in spite of acknowledging the extent of my supporting research.

And it appears to depend a lot on the initial attitude a critic has toward a review when he sets the stage. What kind of a job does he mean to do? What taste does he plan to leave in the mouth of the reader? A Utah reviewer, it seems, took hold of a sharp stick as his method of communication and poked it in all directions. He said it would not be kind to indicate all my flaws—and then proceeded to list a great number of them. Maybe it relieved his dyspepsia.

Another aspect of this "lack of vision" is a tendency, perhaps a desire, to keep the impression of Chaucer unchanged. His reputation and his writings are often treated as if they are carved in stone.

Some ideas "discovered" in my research had been around for years, but I didn't know that. For example, I felt the information about the lawyer who wrote, in the 1940s, regarding Chaucer's rape case had been ignored. Not so. The academic community knew all about it, but I had never heard it discussed in courses I took, nor mentioned in Chaucer texts I'd used. The subject and the medieval explication came as a surprise and were as fresh, to me, as *primary* research.

Then there is the matter of my ingenuity, which is not mine but my recognition of Chaucer's. It is not always well received, and often made short work of. For example, a Cambridge don, who played the little sleuthing game, said he admired my inquiring mind, but.... When he saw the solution to the game, so as not to just "fob me off," he listed eleven areas of refutation to my solution, all of which supported the standard view. Mind you, he did this without seeing a crumb of my evidence.

Chaucer's words are my passion, which is why the *Middle English Dictionary* means so much to me. I really can't help myself. His quirky terms, his peculiar choices, his double entendres, fascinate me. *Blankmanger*, for instance, can be seen as *white manger* and, in addition, *The Manger* is the name of a star cluster in the sign of Cancer. A reviewer who chose to define that white manger as a "cattle stall" instead, thereby nullified the starry image. Her point of view cuts off the relation to Chaucer's other zodiac clues. Chaucer's entertaining double entendre points to the identifying star cluster on one level, and a pudding on the second level. The pudding is "made" by the Cook. *Made* by the Cook because it is *part* of the Cook, as the starry Manger is part of the sign of Cancer. To substitute "cattle" turns all eyes toward the pasture, and allows only an earthbound connection.

Continuing to speak of words, I had a rare opportunity to learn the scholarly attitude toward a troublesome (for me) little word. I found myself in a room full of professors and graduate students at a Chaucer conference, and took the opportunity to ask a question about the Thopas story. "Why, in these days when obscenity is accepted and even encouraged, why, when Chaucer says 'pricking' do the notes continue to advise, as they have for generations, that he means *galloping* or *spurring*?" (Pricking is the main activity in the story. Everyone in the room knew that.) One older gentleman allowed that the word may not have been a sexual referent when Chaucer lived. (The MED offers *intercourse* as a possibility.) Beyond his comment, no one had any more to say. How disappointing. How status quo. *Galloping* surely dulls down the flavor of the potentially spicy *Tale*. And, oddly enough, the horse and horse riding are a sexual convention dating back to biblical times. Pilgrim Chaucer does *not* tell an exceedingly foolish story, as is generally maintained. Instead, he tells the raciest story in the collection.

My using the remarkable, recently completed MED (instead of the *Oxford English Dictionary*, printed in its finished form in the 1920s) is questioned. It is complained that I'm only searching for words that fit my ideas. Well, yes. Should researchers be limited to definitions that come to mind first because we feel most comfortable with them, with words we already know? I love to saunter through the pages of the MED to catch a glimpse of interesting strangers among medieval definitions. Sometimes more than one definition fits Chaucer's line; the effect can be dramatic, mind-boggling. Here's just one instance: *fonde*. Definition 7 says "to strive, to endeavor"; but definition 1 says "to try the patience of God." The contrast *is* mind-boggling. And even more so, Chaucer's line can be read with either meaning; the intent is dramatically different. One definition fits the surface story, the other advances the hidden message. Together they add stature to Chaucer's genius.

A question often asked is, "What has happened to the general reader of Chaucer?" Nostalgia is expressed for the time when reading Chaucer meant simply enjoying his stories, where the reader of pre-professional Chaucerianism did not aim at study or analysis. His appeal to the average reader with curiosity is reflected in my own impressions—how I see Chaucer, and how I see the efforts of academe. Appeal to general readers could be encouraged by the movie "The Knight's Tale" (where Chaucer is one of the characters). And Terry Jones' well-documented "inquest" (*Who Murdered Chaucer?*), concerned with all questions surrounding Chaucer's death, is an absorbing, surprisingly substantial, effort. Is this the beginning of a trend?

Let's not fail to add the opinion of Father Tom Welbers, who is a prime example of that sought-after general reader. (Father Tom opened our big celebration to the public.) In a column comparing the Chaucer books with the *Da Vinci Code*, he finds my writing "engaging" and says (in print and on the web) that my "wonderful trilogy" is a "serious but fascinating investigation into hidden meanings cloaked in allegory."

Then, finally, there is an informative closing note. A Melbourne scholar does a service by her insight regarding academic reception of the three Chaucer books. My interspersing details of frustrations and successes, she explains, would normally be deleted by an editor. Therefore, she continues, because personal reactions appear in my books, few teachers will recommend them or refer to them in print. So be it. There was no other way to tell *my* story, to record my *adventure*.

I believe that you can get excited about what you find in old books, or new books, and I believe it's all right to say so. No. It isn't just "all right," it's part of the truth. If a fact, or an image, or the beauty of a line—or of a word—quickens something inside of you, stimulates your imagination, takes on a life of its own and leads you where you've never gone before, then, I think, to fail to say so is only telling half the truth.

What I have written is labeled "literary criticism." If I had my druthers I'd call it "literary *adventure*." *Adventure* gets closer to the eagerness and discovery and capturing of a prize that I've experienced. Chaucer's images are so enthralling that, even with disappointments, I didn't see how I could lose interest. I never have.

Others did not feel the same. As I've described, when a door opened just a crack, and light streamed out from within, academic bystanders showed no interest in discovering what wonders might be found inside! At the beginning, that was mainly my fault because of my inability to provide a clear picture of the vast complexity of Chaucer's creation. The San Dimas writers' group has been an inestimable assistance in my learning to explain.

To change the pre-existing impression of the poet and his purpose, for many academics, is well-nigh impossible. Maybe a statement from Max Planck, Nobel prize-winning physicist, fits the situation in which I find myself: "A new truth does not triumph by convincing its opponents and making them see the light, but rather because its opponents eventually die, and a new generation grows up that is familiar with it." As we wait upon that "new generation," we can't allow the force working to remove early literature to succeed.

It is not only the U.S., not only the West Coast, that feels the strong force that concerned Professor Dick Barnes. In England, Professor Brewer had similar thoughts. "There is at present a dominant anti-historic and anti-literary element in our culture," he states, which contrasts with a "rage for the contemporary." I can see this creating an isolating barrier beyond which the student will not be expected to venture.

If, because of this, Chaucer is allowed to fade into the dim past, if colleges and universities remove his works from their curriculums, we will have lost a world of Chaucer's thoughts that lie waiting to be explored. His messages will languish undiscovered.

Any activity counteracting medieval literature's demise holds an element of hope. Where Chaucer remains a subject of study, teachers who are "creative" often encourage their classes to see Chaucer functioning in today's world:

Who is your favorite Pilgrim? Why? Which actor would play that part staged as a Hollywood movie?

Choose three women from the Tales and construct a case against their husbands for spousal abuse.

If the Pilgrims were transported in cars instead of by horses, describe the car each would drive.

All of the above may arouse student interest. Novel teaching methods, that aim at making Chaucer appear "with it," can amuse young people with their own ingenuity. And, while I acknowledge such activities do add the quality of a real human being to the poet, none of it deals with honest-to-goodness Chaucer, or his purpose. Will such techniques connect, at some later date, to serious investigation with a deeper regard for the poet in the medieval milieu? Who can say? At least, one can hope that such classroom methods will keep the name of Chaucer alive for a growing audience.

For the average reader Chaucer's writings rendered in Modern English can be captivating, can demonstrate his inventiveness and diversity. Along with reading, a general audience is attracted to the *Tales* and their author through movies, TV adaptations, and animated productions, as well as through books about his life—and death. All such entertainments keep his name in the public eye. And, stretching our imagination, the *Canterbury Tales* can currently be found as *rap!* The young Canadian, Baba Brinkman, has performed his hip-hop version to Canadian audiences, as well as in the U.K., Australia, and the hallowed halls of Harvard. Who knows how widespread Chaucer's popularity could become? There is undeniable appeal to his work on many levels.

In my personal effort to promote the circulation of Chaucer's name, I continued to create T-shirts. The first two were fun, and I found they stimulated *Chaucer* as a topic of conversation. So I designed a series of shirts. The most popular says "The lyf so short, the craft so long to lerne." (The thought of life being short, and one's craft difficult to learn also gives *me* pause.) The runner-up in popularity displays the logo for CelebrateChaucer.com. And, of course, there is a shirt that sports the opening lines of the *General Prologue*—"Whan that Aprill…" on the back. The words are frequently recited aloud by customers behind me in line at the grocery store, the post office, or wherever.

You can also find the logo blazoned across the computer screen at my Chaucer website. The website was launched at the prompting of Charles Goldsmid, friend and advisor, in addition to being the former proprietor of Claremont's eclectic, second-floor bookshop. A grandson of mine, with the appropriate talents, did the construction of the site. Many important facets of recent Chaucer episodes are recorded there, including photos and videos of our annual October 25th event.

For a simple way of acquainting people with Chaucer, I've created many information sheets and celebratory bookmarks which are distributed when I give a talk about Chaucer. And I talk about Chaucer at every opportunity—to students, ladies' clubs, church groups, or libraries. A short time ago the local Comcast TV station interviewed me. The tape aired soon after and, serendipitously, is resuscitated at unpredictable intervals, which pleases me no end.

Keeping Chaucer's name alive has a parallel aspect of importance—the continued reading of Middle English. There is a tendency to use texts in Modern English which provide no challenge to the reader. His poetry in the English of today is fine, even recommended, for the dilettante. But the fact must be noted that, although modern adaptations may be entertaining, it is not Chaucer who is the entertainer.

With all that has already been recognized, as concealed in Chaucer's lines, how much more needs to be brought to the surface? If Middle English is bypassed in school, how will the wonders be found? Who will find them?

Because students—and others—fear even *trying* to read English of the fourteenth century, I wrote a little book partly to amuse, partly to encourage—*Who's Afraid of Middle English?* The several thousand words it contains are all Middle English, and all the words are readily readable for us today. Carrying the "fearful" idea to the back cover, you'll find the story of the "three litel pigges" and the "bigge, badde wolfe."

I gaze across a vast pool of information. It's rewarding to see several buoys I've launched each sporting a slender pennant that proclaims CELEBRATE CHAUCER—the beginning and the end of my inspiration.

IX.

Retro-Revelation!

LET'S TAKE A BRIEF backward glance at 1994. That's when my Good Samaritan friend Viola introduced me to the San Dimas writers' group. She also introduced me to an article by Carolyn Heilbrun. The article had inspired Viola to tell about her life in the organization called "Moral Rearmament," and how it had shaped her future. When I read Heilbrun's words they confirmed for me a plan to organize my insight into Chaucer and get it down on paper. The message we read exhorted older women who have a level of financial security to speak out when they recognize something that needs to be said. *Take risks; make noise; be courageous; don't hesitate to become unpopular.* The words were a call to action.

At the time, I needed nothing more from Heilbrun. But, about a year ago, I had a desire to get better acquainted with her thinking. Half a dozen of her books were readily available. (She also wrote a series of murder mysteries under the name Amanda Cross, but that's another story.) I borrowed several Heilbrun books from the city library. As I read them, my view of the world—the college world—evolved, became transfigured.

You may remember that I had been raised in the big city, but when I entered college I certainly was naïve, or at least uninformed. Heilbrun made it clear that I had lived my college years wearing blinders, not *really* aware of what went on around me. My mental image of school and of teachers had not changed since my adolescence. School was my favorite place to be, and teachers were my heroes.

Admiration for educators crossed the threshold with me into college. It did not change in spite of the *dissuasion* I encountered. Confused, and plagued by the feeling of being an "intellectual

[147]

bottleneck," I would tell myself, perhaps I'm just not capable. Heilbrun not only removed my blinders, but lighted the path I had traveled. What I had perceived as pale, shapeless obstacles are now distinct; reality has darker colors and sharper edges.

A thumbnail sketch of Professor Carolyn G. Heilbrun will help you understand how her recommendation could be so meaningful to both Viola and me. Heilbrun had entered Columbia University's graduate school as a brilliant young woman, who, upon receiving her doctorate, joined the faculty of the Columbia English Department. When given tenure, she made history as the first woman to gain such a position there. Then, after thirty years, came her test of courage and integrity. In 1992, as a woman in her sixties, having considerable security from her own income and that of her husband, she publicly demonstrated her convictions. With no alternative but to take an unpopular stand on an academic issue, she resigned her position. She stood by her principles even though it meant an end to her career. Chaucer would have said she taught, but first and last she followed the teaching herself.

As I read her books, I began to understand the reasons behind what had happened to me. My comparison will be brief; the connections still surprise me.

Let's begin by being direct. Trite, but true: *It's a man's world.* You may have seen this from the start as the cause of my difficulty, but it took Heilbrun to show me where I stood.

Though this first illustration will seem straight out of the Victorian era, it comes from mid-twentieth century. A friend of Heilbrun's—a woman—had a poem rejected for publication. The reason? Not because it lacked literary merit, but because the journal in question had published a poem *by a woman* in the previous issue!

In Heilbrun's field of specialization, Modern British Literature, all the authors studied were men—with the token exception of Jane Austen. When she raised the question of including other female authors, her idea proved *laughable* to the men of the faculty.

Heilbrun also observed that *particular* students encouraged as "disciples" of one of the outstanding scholars in the English department, were all, without exception, young men. You may remember that Virginia Adair, in a note to me, referred to "the Big Boys." That was no accidental phrase. That was the college world.

Now that I am informed, it no longer surprises me that Professor Elliott, Professor Chorney, and Professor Ware were all less than encouraging. No, let's make that *downright discouraging*. Not only was I a woman, but a gray-haired mother-figure. They did their best to put me in my proper place, the place reserved for women.

When the following incident occurred, I could not understand why Professor Lillian Wilds, who had recently received her Ph.D., had shown my ideas to her advisor from graduate school. The explanation seems simple now. Dr. Wilds had not acquired the confidence associated with a doctorate. She looked to a man's judgment to be sure of *her* opinion.

That covers my *personal* experience. Now, how do Heilbrun's disclosures relate to the *Chaucer* experience? Her observations about English studies, both the analysis of literature and the teaching of it, are a revelation.

"The tyranny of academic fashion" is a phrase I scribbled down a couple of years ago, because, when I read it, it so concisely captured the unbending atmosphere of denial toward articles about Chaucer I had tried to publish.

Heilbrun addresses this "academic fashion." I am amused by her illustration in "Bring the Spirit Back to English Studies" (1979). She prods faculty members, "Let us admit that English studies are in the doldrums. What I really believe is that they are in a state it would be meiotic [rhetorically understated] to call parlous [perilous], but doldrums will do." I'm sure you've seen the quip, "Never use a big word when a diminuitive one will do." She makes it tauntingly obvious, here, that a simple, homey word conveys her message, but in using it an author would be thought less of by colleagues.

After her retirement, Heilbrun laments she has lost her taste for literary criticism, partly because of its overblown vocabulary, but also because it seems a far cry from the works it "pretends to illuminate." "Pretends" is a provocative, a courageous, word for her to use there. She sees professors of English wearily choosing between teaching "the same old stuff" or else digging into new theories that are concealed "in a thicket of language so dense as to be virtually impenetrable." She detests the old methods, reading the same books, asking the same questions. In order to "restore excitement to the classroom," she advises challenging the ordinary "assumptions" about "masterpieces." I could not agree more. The essentials, I believe, are to aim for clarity, use language easily understood by the average intelligent person, and challenge old assumptions. That's my plan for getting to the heart of Chaucer's "masterpiece."

And, for a final connection, she says (in *The Last Gift of Time*) she had been trained "to regard the personal as inadmissible" in literary analysis. Such training echoed, many years later, in comments from Australia, where the professor said inclusion of my personal remarks disallowed recommending my Chaucer books. My feeling is that such training removes the human touch from criticism. Why should students *not* be told how a researcher/ scholar feels about his topic, his specialty? It could forge a link to a *human* voice and fire a student's imagination!

Thinking of that sought-after general reader, I can't imagine the ordinary reader indulging in essays with "impenetrable new theories." And the result of a "pretense" of illumination might actually be negative, not being enlightened but befogged instead. Challenging the dusty old assumptions holds excitement. What would there be to lose? Think of the enthusiasm that might be gained in searching for corroborating evidence.

It is my fond hope that academe will peep out from beneath the cumbersome blanket of scholarly vocabulary and style to see literature with a lively simplicity, a different point of view rather than simply years-old tradition. Heilbrun helped me to account for academic reactions I had faced. The past has not changed, but my *commitment* for the future is renewed, because, as Goethe says, there is "Power and Magic in it." I have nothing to lose, and I have a cause about which I am still passionate.

X.

What Now—and Why?

CHAUCER'S CONTEMPORARIES, including royalty, recognized his writing skill. His words have a liveliness. Something is agitating beneath the surface, even in his early works. The first long poem we have, *The Book of the Duchess*, has a snippet that revealed a small but surprising significance to a reader in the 1800s. The words *A long castle with walls white, By Saint John, on a rich hill* refer to the names Lancaster, Blanche, John of Gaunt, and Richmond. These are persons and places meaningful in Chaucer's life and in the life of fourteenth-century England. Can you see this as a seedling of what would come to full bloom in the *Canterbury Tales*, his last and most exquisitely complex work?

Quickly scanning only the titles of two other poems, *Parlement of Foules* can be wordplay for *the chattering of fools*. These fools/fowls meet annually. (Which annual gathering might be seen as the useless debate of fools?) *House of Fame* can point to a *famous house*, a house where men's reputations are said to be preserved or destroyed by whim. (What sort of "house" had such power?) With the setting aside of standard impression unseen alternate images can surface.

The ambiguity in those titles makes me see him working and improving, until he envisioned the intricate plan for the *Canterbury Tales*, his ultimate creation. I am convinced, as well, that each of his previous works has a layer of meaning waiting to be discovered. That's the reason I feel that a continued interest in Chaucer is paramount. One isolated detail at a time may seem unimportant, but collectively multiple details are the fabric of a network discernible below the surface.

It is one thing for scholars to have a clear understanding of the rhythm of the lines, the derivation of the words, the source of the chosen analogue, and more. But it is another for them to express expertise in terms that a broad, rather than a narrow, audience can appreciate. The average reader would not enjoy many interpretive essays concerning Chaucer. Criticism written with a wide audience in mind could acquaint the reader with a depth of the poet's genius, and perhaps a more penetrating view of his times.

Over the last century, much research regarding Chaucer and the fourteenth century has been published. A new spirit of research/criticism dedicated to acknowledging a hidden intent is the invitation extended toward lively investigation. This can open a whole new vista for the study, the research, the criticism, the evaluation of a hidden interpretation. A parallel universe exists in Chaucer's poetry. Who will venture to go there? Perhaps it will be young scholars. Judy Wenrick's blurb for the second book (*Pilgrim Chaucer*) recommends that it "serves as a teaching model to inspire writing students to view scholarship as an adventurous and creative endeavor."

Chaucer's use of words is my never-ending fascination. Among writers of his day, the poet had a reputation as expert with subtle and covert words. His way of referring to *ambiguity* is *double words sly, such as men call a word with two faces*. In his translation of the *Romance of the Rose*, the most famous allegory of the Middle Ages, he speaks of *double sentence* which is understood as *double meaning*. The challenge of perceiving a second level of meaning in allegory entertained medieval readers. The covert element was seen as a prize won through effort. Although the word order is archaic, in Chaucer's following comment we see him encouraging his readership with a pat on the back: whoever has the subtlety (the skill) a *double sentence* will see. A reward awaits the skillful person who will search his allegories.

And what would be the purpose of his *double sentence?* As I said much earlier, Chaucer knew the critical messages he enclosed put his life at risk. There are words, phrases, scenes in the *Tales* with little or no apparent "meaning." I believe we simply have not penetrated their purpose. Recall that Virginia Adair knew, instinctively, that the dreadful wife of the Host (that is, of Christ) had to be *the Church*. A phantom image of inquisitorial practices lurks within the portrait of the Host's wife. It took genius on the part of the poet to avoid suspicion, to escape detection. His courage and keen wit drive me to want to tell his story.

An additional intriguing mystery is worth pondering. How were Chaucer's works preserved? The manuscripts we have were all created *after his death*. How strange. What happened to his personal "papers," or the original copies—and why? Such considerations intensify my fascination with Chaucer. A rental agreement is evidence that he moved to lodgings at Westminster Abbey in June 1400. With no interim disclosures, we are told he died in October. (Terry Jones' recent *Who Murdered Chaucer?* is a serious and lengthy inquiry into possibilities.) No details of those last months are recorded, no hint about daily activities, no cause of death, no explanation of any final arrangements. Instead, a haunting question remains. Who managed to have the existing manuscripts created and preserved? Chaucer had friends very near the crown. He had entertained the court with his writings—and his readings. Some of his poetry was "commissioned" by nobility. An additional question is: when the copies that exist today were completed, then what happened to Chaucer's "papers"? It surely is mysterious that they had not been safeguarded as part of an historic treasure as are the writings of lesser authors of his day.

Through the years, my mind has been occupied with more than garden mulch and cookie dough. Never doubt that a great deal of thinking goes on, even—maybe especially—while a woman washes dishes! Some of my pursuits have been successes, while others still await solutions. What a task to anticipate! Consider, for example, that while contemplating the Pilgrim Knight, I perceived a projection beyond anything I had seen before. Always searching for that *second* intention, this was different. An awesome vision of a *third* dimension is unmistakable. My question, then, is—are there *three* allegorical levels to be found? It would not be unheard of in medieval allegory. If I had another life to live, I would pick up from here and enlarge everything I've done. But, in any case, I'll use the life I have left, for as long as it lasts, to rejoice in the tantalizing possibilities.

I love to think about the animated reaction of students and audiences, the spark of recognition at the moment when they, too, saw the double images. Once in a while, I feel a little sad for the professors who failed to participate in the excitement. And I am truly grateful for required courses. If I hadn't been "forced" to study Chaucer, I would have missed the intellectual adventure of a lifetime.

At age thirty, I hiked the Grand Canyon. It was the most remarkable personal adventure I'd had up to that time. But the universe Chaucer has created far surpasses the wonders of the Canyon. Describing his "universe" is, I believe, the "something special" I felt I would do. Carolyn Heilbrun speaks of women who have a sense of "destiny." Perhaps that is a more elegant way of saying the same thing.

My teenagers

My amazement and enthusiasm began when I was the mother of teenagers. Now that I am the great-grandmother of ten (or more, by the time you read this), my thrill over Chaucer has not diminished. A great deal of my thinking goes on in the freedom outside the box. But carelessness is not tolerated. I'm careful with my "homework." Why not? That's where the fun, the excitement begins and thrives.

I've told a lot of that story. It's gratifying that the extent of my research has been noted. It has also been said that there is no question I've made interesting connections. My thoughts are considered "unconventional," and that's the way it ought to be. Those marvelous double images in my head are unlike any other portraits of Chaucer's Pilgrims. The celestial concept has been called fun and a fresh new look—a *must* read. Could I ask for more? My scholarly work and extensive notes (which you may feel free to skip, if you prefer) are an invitation into a world fashioned six centuries ago, but only opened to the public in the last ten years. My books are the ticket to that world.

Bon voyage!

THE END

MY CHILDREN

Mari

Ted

Marge

Catherine

MY GRANDCHILDREN

Mike *Rebecca* *Matt*

Rachel *Gabby*

Rosanna *Andy* *Michelle*

MY GREAT-GRANDCHILDREN

Emily *Abigail* *Xavier*

Olivia *J.J.*

Zach *Max* *Fionn*

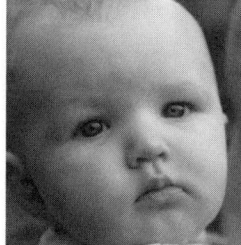 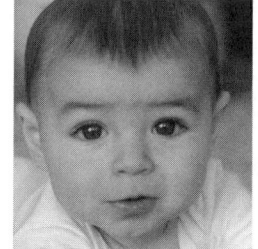

Sabrina *Drew*